COMUS

JOHN MILTON

COMUS

EDITED BY

A. W. VERITY, M.A.

CAMBRIDGE
AT THE UNIVERSITY PRESS
1921

CAMBRIDGE
UNIVERSITY PRESS

University Printing House, Cambridge CB2 8BS, United Kingdom

Cambridge University Press is part of the University of Cambridge.

It furthers the University's mission by disseminating knowledge in the pursuit of education, learning and research at the highest international levels of excellence.

www.cambridge.org
Information on this title: www.cambridge.org/9781316633373

© Cambridge University Press 1921

First edition 1909
Reprinted 1909, 1912 (twice), 1913, 1914, 1921
First paperback edition 2016

A catalogue record for this publication is available from the British Library

ISBN 978-1-316-63337-3 Paperback

NOTE.

THIS volume is partly a recast of the earlier editions of this poem in the "Pitt Press Series," and I desire to repeat my acknowledgment of indebtedness to other Editors.

I have also the pleasure to thank the General Editor of the series for many valuable suggestions.

A. W. V.

CONTENTS.

INTRODUCTION.

LIFE OF MILTON.

MILTON'S life falls into three clearly defined divisions.
The first period ends with the poet's return *The three*
from Italy in 1639; the second at the *periods in*
Restoration in 1660, when release from the *Milton's life.*
fetters of politics enabled him to remind the world that
he was a great poet, if not a great controversialist; the
third is brought to a close with his death in 1674. The
poems given in the present volume date from the first of
these periods; but we propose to summarise briefly the
main events of all three.

John Milton was born on December 9, 1608, in
London. He came, in his own words, *ex*   *Born 1608;*
genere honesto. A family of Miltons had *the poet's*
been settled in Oxfordshire since the reign *father.*
of Elizabeth. The poet's father had been educated at an
Oxford school, possibly as a chorister in one of the
College choir-schools, and imbibing Anglican sympathies
had conformed to the Established Church. For this he
was disinherited by his father, a Roman Catholic. He
settled in London, as a scrivener. A scrivener com-
bined the occupations of lawyer and law-stationer. It
appears to have been a lucrative calling; certainly
John Milton (the poet was named after the father)
attained to easy circumstances. He married about 1600,
and had six children, of whom several died young. The
third child was the poet.

The elder Milton was evidently a man of considerable
culture, in particular an accomplished musician, and a
composer whose madrigals were deemed worthy of being

printed side by side with those of Byrd, Orlando Gibbons and other leading musicians of the time. To him, no doubt, the poet owed the love of music of which we see frequent indications in the poems. Realising, too, that in his son lay the promise and possibility of future greatness, John Milton took the utmost pains to have the boy adequately educated; and the lines *Ad Patrem* show that the ties of affection between father and child were of more than ordinary closeness.

Milton was sent to St Paul's School about the year *Early Training.* 1620. Here two influences, apart from those of ordinary school-life, may have affected him particularly. The headmaster was a good English scholar; he published a grammar containing many extracts from English poets, notably Spenser; it is reasonable to assume that he had not a little to do with the encouragement and guidance of Milton's early taste for English poetry. Also, the founder of St Paul's School, Colet, had prescribed as part of the school-course the study of certain early Christian writers, whose influence is said to be directly traceable in Milton's poems and may in some cases have suggested his choice of sacred themes. While at St Paul's, Milton also had a tutor at home, Thomas Young, a Scotchman, afterwards an eminent Puritan divine—the inspirer, doubtless, of much of his pupil's Puritan sympathies. And Milton enjoyed the signal advantage of growing up in the stimulating atmosphere of cultured home-life. Most men do not realise that the word 'culture' signifies anything very definite or desirable before they pass to the University; for Milton, however, home-life meant, from the first, not only broad interests and refinement, but active encouragement towards literature and study. In 1625 he left St Paul's. Of his extant English poems only one, *On the Death of a Fair Infant*, dates from his school-days; but we are told that he had written much verse, English and Latin. And his early training had done that which was all-important: it had laid the

foundation of the far-ranging knowledge which makes
Paradise Lost unique for diversity of suggestion and
interest.

Milton went to Christ's College, Cambridge, in the
Easter term of 1625, took his B.A. degree in *At*
1629, proceeded M.A. in 1632, and in the *Cambridge.*
latter year left Cambridge. The popular view of Milton's
connection with the University will be coloured for all
time by Johnson's unfortunate story that for some
unknown offence he "suffered the public indignity of
corporal correction." For various reasons this story is
now discredited by the best judges. It is certain,
however, that early in 1626 Milton did have some serious
difficulty with his tutor, which led to his removal from
Cambridge for a few weeks and his transference to
another tutor on his return later in the term. He spoke
of the incident bitterly at the time in one of his Latin
poems.

On the other hand he voluntarily passed seven years
at the University, and resented strongly the imputation
brought against him in the "Smectymnuus" controversy
that he had been in ill-favour with the authorities of his
college. Writing in 1642, he takes the opportunity "to
acknowledge publicly with all grateful mind, that more
than ordinary favour and respect, which I found above
any of my equals at the hands of those courteous and
learned men, the fellows of that college wherein I spent
some years : who at my parting, after I had taken two
degrees, as the manner is, signified many ways how much
better it would content them that I would stay ; as by
many letters full of kindness and loving respect, both
before that time, and long after, I was assured of their
singular good affection towards me." And if we look
into those uncomplimentary allusions to Cambridge
which date from the controversial period of his life we
see that the feeling they represent is hardly more than a
phase of his theological bias. He detested ecclesiasticism,
and for him the two Universities (there is a fine im-

partiality in his diatribes) are the strongholds of what
he detested : "nurseries of superstition"—"not yet well
recovered from the scholastic grossness of barbarous
ages"—given up to "monkish and miserable sophistry,"
and unprogressive in their educational methods. But it
may fairly be assumed that Milton the scholar and poet,
who chose to spend seven years at Cambridge, owed to
her more than Milton the fierce controversialist admitted
or knew. A poet he had proved himself before leaving
the University in 1632. The short but exquisite ode
At a Solemn Music, and the *Nativity Hymn* (1629), were
already written.

Milton's father had settled[1] at Horton in Buckingham-
The five   shire. Thither the son retired in 1632. He
years (1632—   had gone to Cambridge with the intention of
1637) *spent at*   qualifying for some profession, perhaps the
Horton.   Church[2]. This purpose was soon given up,
and when Milton returned to his father's house he seems
to have made up his mind that there was no profession
which he cared to enter. He would choose the better
part of studying and preparing himself, by rigorous self-
discipline and application, for the far-off divine event to
which his whole life moved.

It was Milton's constant resolve to achieve something

[1] As tenant of the Earl of Bridgewater, according to one
account; but probably the tradition arose from Milton's subsequent connection with the Bridgewater family.

[2] Cf. Milton's own words, "The Church, to whose service
by the intention of my parents and friends I was destined of a
child, and in my own resolutions." What kept him from taking
orders was not, at first, any difference of belief, but solely his
objection to Church discipline and government. "Coming to
some maturity of years, and perceiving what tyranny had invaded
in the church, that he who would take orders must subscribe
slave......(I) thought it better to prefer a blameless silence before
the sacred office of speaking, bought and begun with servitude
and forswearing."—*Reason of Church Government*, P. W. II.
482. Milton disliked in particular the episcopal system, and
spoke of himself as "Church-outed by the prelates.'

that should vindicate the ways of God to men, something
great[1] that should justify his own possession   *The key to
of unique powers—powers of which, with no   Milton's life.*
trace of egotism, he proclaims himself proudly conscious.
The feeling finds repeated expression in his prose ; it
is the guiding-star that shines clear and steadfast even
through the mists of politics. He has a mission to fulfil,
a purpose to accomplish, no less than the most earnest
of religious enthusiasts ; and the means whereby this
end is to be attained are fourfold : devotion to learning, devotion to religion, ascetic purity of life, and
the pursuit of σπουδαιότης or "excellent seriousness" of
thought.

This period of self-centred isolation lasted from 1632
to 1637. Gibbon tells us among the many wise things
contained in that most wise book the *Autobiography*,
that every man has two educations : that which he
receives from his teachers and that which he owes to
himself; the latter being often the more important.
During these five years Milton completed his second
education ; ranging the whole world of classical antiquity
and absorbing the classical genius so thoroughly that the
ancients were to him what they afterwards became to
Landor, what they have perhaps never become to any other
English poet in the same degree, even as the very breath
of his being ; learning, too, all of art, especially music,
that contemporary England could furnish; wresting from
modern languages and literatures their last secrets ; and
combining these vast and diverse influences into a
splendid equipment of hard-won, well-ordered culture.

[1] Cf. the second sonnet; "How soon hath Time." Ten
years later (1641) Milton speaks of the "inward prompting
which grows daily upon me, that by labour and intent study,
which I take to be my portion in this life, joined with the strong
propensity of nature, I might perhaps leave something so written
to after times, as they should not willingly let it die"—*Reason
of Church Government, P. IV.* ii. 477, 478.

The world has known many greater scholars in the technical, limited sense than Milton, but few men, if any, who have mastered more things worth mastering in art, letters and scholarship[1]. It says much for the poet that he was sustained through this period of study, pursued *ohne Hast, ohne Rast*, by the full consciousness that all would be crowned by a masterpiece which should add one more testimony to the belief in that God who ordains the fates of men. It says also a very great deal for the father who suffered his son to follow in this manner the path of learning[2].

True, Milton gave more than one earnest of his future *Milton's lyric verse; its relation to contemporary life.* fame. The dates of the early pieces— *L'Allegro, Il Penseroso, Arcades, Comus* and *Lycidas*—are not all certain; but probably each was composed at Horton before 1638. We must speak of them elsewhere. Here we may note that four of them have great autobiographic value as an indirect commentary, written from Milton's coign of seclusion, upon the moral crisis through which English life and thought were passing, the clash between the careless, pleasure-seeking Cavalier world and the deepening austerity of Puritanism. In *L'Allegro* the poet holds the balance almost equal between the two opposing tendencies. In *Il Penseroso* it becomes clear to which side his sympathies are leaning. *Comus* is a covert prophecy of the downfall of the Court-party, while *Lycidas* openly "foretells the ruine" of the Established Church. The latter poem is the final utterance of Milton's lyric genius.

---

[1] Milton's poems with their undercurrent of perpetual allusion are the best proof of the width of his reading; but interesting supplementary evidence is afforded by the commonplace book discovered in 1874, and printed by the *Camden Society*, 1876. It contains extracts from about 80 different authors whose works Milton had studied.

[2] Cf. the poem *Ad Patrem*, 68—72, in which Milton thanks his father for not having forced him to be a merchant or lawyer.

Here he reaches, in Mr Mark Pattison's words, the high-water mark of English verse ; and then—the pity of it—he resigns his place among poets, gives himself up to politics, and for nearly twenty years suffers his lyre to hang mute and rusty in the temple of the Muses.

The composition of *Lycidas* may be assigned to the year 1637. In the spring of the next year *Travels in* Milton started for Italy. He had long made *Italy; close* himself a master of Italian, and it was *period in his* natural that he should seek inspiration in *life.* the land where many English poets, from Chaucer to Shelley, have found it. Milton remained abroad some fifteen months. Originally he had intended to include Sicily and Greece in his travels, but news of the troubles in England hastened his return. He was brought face to face with the question whether or not he *Cause of* should bear his part in the coming struggle ; *his return to* whether without self-reproach he could lead *England.* any longer this life of learning and indifference to the public weal. He decided as we might have expected that he would decide, though some good critics see cause to regret the decision. Milton puts his position very clearly. " I considered it," he says, " dishonourable to be enjoying myself at my ease in foreign lands, while my countrymen were striking a blow for freedom." And again : " Perceiving that the true way to liberty followed on from these beginnings, inasmuch also as I had so prepared myself from my youth that, above all things, I could not be ignorant what is of Divine and what of human right, I resolved, though I was then meditating certain other matters, to transfer into this struggle all my genius and all the strength of my industry."

The summer of 1639 (July) found Milton back in England. Immediately after his return he *The second* wrote the *Epitaphium Damonis*, the beautiful *period, 1639—* elegy in which he lamented the death of his *1660. Milton* *abandons poe-* school friend, Diodati. *Lycidas* was the last *try.*

of the English lyrics: the *Epitaphium*, which should be studied in close connection with *Lycidas*, the last of the long Latin poems. Thenceforth, for a long spell, the rest was silence, so far as concerned poetry. The period which for all men represents the strength and maturity of manhood, which in the cases of other poets produces the best and most characteristic work, is with Milton a blank. In twenty years he composed no more than a bare handful of Sonnets, and even some of these are infected by the taint of political *animus*. Other interests filled his thoughts—the question of Church-reform, education, marriage, and, above all, politics.

Pamphlets on the Church and Education. Milton's first treatise upon the government of the Established Church (*Of Reformation touching Church-Discipline in England*) appeared in 1641. Others followed in quick succession. The abolition of Episcopacy was the watchword of the enemies of the Anglican Church—the great rallying-cry of Puritanism, and no one enforced the point with greater eloquence than Milton. During 1641 and 1642 he wrote five pamphlets on the subject. Meanwhile he was studying the principles of education. On his return from Italy he had undertaken the training of his nephews[1]. This led to consideration of the best educational methods; and in the *Tractate on Education*, 1644, Milton assumed the part of educational theorist.

Marriage. In the previous year, May, 1643, he married[2]. The marriage proved, at the time, unfortunate. Its immediate outcome was the pamphlets on

[1] Edward and John Phillips, sons of Milton's only sister. Both subsequently joined the Royalist party. To Edward Phillips we owe a memoir of the poet.

[2] His wife (who was only seventeen) was Mary Powell, eldest daughter of Richard Powell, of Forest Hill, a village some little distance from Oxford. She went to stay with her father in July 1643, and refused to return to Milton; why, it is not certain. She was reconciled to her husband in 1645, bore him four children, and died in 1652, in her twenty-seventh year.

Divorce. Clearly he had little leisure for literature proper.

The finest of Milton's prose works, *Areopagitica*, a plea for the free expression of opinion, was *Political Pamphlets.* published in 1644. In 1645[1] he edited the *Appointment* first collection of his poems. In 1649 his *to Latin Se-cretaryship.* advocacy of the anti-royalist cause was recognised by the offer of a post under the newly appointed Council of State. His bold vindication of the trial of Charles I., *The Tenure of Kings*, had appeared earlier in the same year. Milton accepted the offer,

---

No doubt, the scene in *Paradise Lost* x. 909—946, in which Eve begs forgiveness of Adam, reproduced the poet's personal experience, while many passages in *Samson Agonistes* must have been inspired by the same cause.

[1] i.e. old style. The volume was entered on the registers of the Stationers' Company under the date of October 6th, 1645. It was published on Jan. 2, 1646, with the following title-page:

"*Poems of Mr. John Milton, both English and Latin, compos'd at several times. Printed by his true Copies. The Songs were set in Musick by Mr. Henry Lawes, gentleman of the King's Chappel, and one of His Majesties private Musick.*

'————*Baccare frontem Cingite, ne vati noceat mala lingua futuro.*' VIRG. *Ecl.* 7.

Printed and publish'd according to Order. London, Printed by Ruth Raworth, for Humphrey Moseley, and are to be sold at the signe of the Princes Arms in Pauls Churchyard. 1645."

From the prefatory Address to the Reader it is clear that the collection was due to the initiative of the publisher. Milton's own feeling is expressed by the motto, where the words "*vati futuro*" show that, as he judged, his great achievement was yet to come. The volume was divided into two parts, the first containing the English, the second the Latin poems. *Comus* was printed at the close of the former, with a separate title-page to mark its importance.

becoming Latin[1] Secretary to the Committee of Foreign
Affairs. There was nothing distasteful about his duties.
He drew up the despatches to foreign governments,
translated state-papers, and served as interpreter to
foreign envoys. Had his duties stopped here his ac-
ceptance of the post would, I think, have proved an
unqualified gain. It brought him into contact with the

*The advan-
tage of the
post.*
first men in the state[2], gave him a practical
insight into the working of national affairs
and the motives of human action; in a word,
furnished him with that experience of life which is essential
to all poets who aspire to be something more than "the idle

*Its disad-
vantage.*
singers of an empty day." But unfortunately
the secretaryship entailed the necessity of
defending at every turn the past course of the revolution
and the present policy of the Council. Milton, in fact,
held a perpetual brief as advocate for his party. Hence
the endless and unedifying controversies into which he
drifted; controversies which wasted the most precious
years of his life, warped, as some critics think, his nature,
and eventually cost him his eyesight.

Between 1649 and 1660 Milton produced no less than

*Milton's
writings on
behalf of the
Common-
wealth.*
eleven pamphlets. Several of these arose out of
the publication of the famous *Eikon Basilike.*
The book was printed in 1649 and created so
great an impression in the king's favour that
Milton was asked to reply to it. This he did with

---

[1] A Latin Secretary was required because the Council scorned,
as Edward Phillips says, "to carry on their affairs in the
wheedling, lisping jargon of the cringing French." Milton's
salary was £288, in modern money about £900.

[2] There is no proof that Milton ever had personal intercourse
with Cromwell, and Mr Mark Pattison implies that he was
altogether neglected by the foremost men of the time. Yet it
seems unlikely that the Secretary of the Committee should not
have been on friendly terms with some of its members, Vane, for
example, and Whitelocke.

Eikonoklastes, introducing the wholly unworthy sneer at Sidney's *Arcadia* and the awkwardly expressed reference to Shakespeare[1]. Controversy of this barren type has the inherent disadvantage that once started it may never end. The Royalists commissioned the Leyden professor, Salmasius, to prepare a counterblast, the *Defensio Regia*, and this in turn was met by Milton's *Pro Populo Anglicano Defensio*, 1651, over the pre- *His blind-* paration of which he lost what little power *ness.* of eyesight remained[2]. Salmasius retorted, and died before his second collection of scurrilities was issued: Milton was bound to answer, and the *Defensio Secunda*

---

[1] See *L'Al.* 133—134, note. It would have been more to the point to remind his readers that the imprisoned king must have spent a good many hours over La Calprenède's *Cassandre*.

[2] Perhaps this was the saddest part of the episode. Milton tells us in the *Defensio Secunda* that his eyesight was injured by excessive study in boyhood: "from the twelfth year of my age I scarce ever left my lessons and went to bed before midnight. This was the first cause of my blindness." Continual reading and writing must have increased the infirmity, and by 1650 the sight of the left eye had gone. He was warned that he must not use the other for book-work. Unfortunately this was just the time when the Commonwealth stood most in need of his services. If Milton had not written the first *Defence* he might have retained his partial vision. The choice lay between private good and public duty. He repeated in 1650 the sacrifice of 1639. "In such a case I could not listen to the physician, not if Æsculapius himself had spoken from his sanctuary; I could not but obey that inward monitor, I know not what, that spoke to me from heaven......I concluded to employ the little remaining eyesight I was to enjoy in doing this, the greatest service to the common weal it was in my power to render" (*Second Defence*). By the Spring of 1652 Milton was quite blind. He was then in his forty-fourth year. The allusion in *Paradise Lost*, III. 21—26, leaves it doubtful from what disease he suffered, whether cataract or amaurosis. Throughout *Samson Agonistes* there are frequent references to his affliction.

appeared in 1654. Neither of the combatants gained anything by the dispute; while the subsequent development of the controversy in which Milton crushed the Amsterdam pastor and professor, Morus, goes far to prove the contention of Mr Mark Pattison, that it was an evil day when the poet left his study at Horton to do battle for the Commonwealth amid the vulgar brawls of the market-place:

> "Not here, O Apollo,
> Were haunts meet for thee."

Fortunately this poetic interregnum in Milton's life was not destined to last much longer. The Restoration came, a blessing in disguise, and in 1660 the ruin of Milton's political party and of his personal hopes, the absolute overthrow of the cause for which he had fought for twenty years, left him free. The author of *Lycidas* could once more become a poet[1].

The Restoration releases Milton from politics. Return to poetry.

Much has been written upon this second period, 1639—1660, and a word may be said here. We saw what parting of the ways confronted Milton on his return from Italy. Did he choose aright? Should he have continued upon the path of learned leisure? There are writers who argue that Milton made a mistake. A poet, they say, should keep clear of political strife: fierce controversy can benefit no man: who touches pitch must expect to be, certainly will be, defiled: Milton sacrificed twenty of the best years of his life, doing work which an underling could have done and which was not

Should Milton have kept apart from political life?

One reply to this question.

---

[1] We have not attempted to trace the growth of Milton's political and religious opinions: "Through all these stages," Mr Mark Pattison writes, "Milton passed in the space of twenty years—Church-Puritan, Presbyterian, Royalist, Independent, Commonwealth's man, Oliverian." To illustrate this statement would need many pages.

worth doing: another *Comus* might have been written, a loftier *Lycidas*: that literature should be the poorer by the absence of these possible masterpieces, that the second greatest genius which England has produced should in a way be the "inheritor of unfulfilled renown," is and must be a thing entirely and terribly deplorable. This is the view of the purely literary critic. Mr Mark Pattison writes very much to this effect.

There remains the other side of the question. It may fairly be contended that had Milton elected *The opposite view.* in 1639 to live the scholar's life apart from "the action of men," *Paradise Lost*, as we have it, could never have been written[1]. Knowledge of life and human nature, insight into the problems of men's motives and emotions, grasp of the broader issues of the human tragedy, all these were essential to the author of an epic poem; they could only be obtained through commerce with the world; they would have remained beyond the reach of a recluse. Dryden complained that Milton saw nature through the spectacles of books: we might have had to complain that he saw men through the same medium. Fortunately it is not so: and it is not so because at the age of twenty-two he threw in his fortunes with those of his country; like the diver in Schiller's ballad he took the plunge which was to cost him so dear. The mere man of letters will never move the world. Æschylus fought at Marathon: Shakespeare was practical to the tips of his fingers; a better business man than Goethe there was not within a radius of a hundred miles of Weimar.

This aspect of the question is emphasised by Milton himself. The man, he says, "who would not *Milton's own opinion.* be frustrate of his hope to write well hereafter in laudable things, ought himself to be a true poem, that is, a composition and pattern of the best and honour-

[1] This is equally true of *Samson Agonistes.*

ablest things, *not*[1] *presuming to sing high praises of heroic men or famous cities, unless he have within himself the experience and the practice of all that which is praise-worthy.*" Again, in estimating the qualifications which the writer of an epic such as he contemplated should possess, he is careful to include "insight into all seemly and generous arts and *affairs*[2]."

Truth usually lies half-way between extremes: perhaps

How politics may have in-fluenced the poet.

it does so here. No doubt, Milton did gain very greatly by breathing awhile the larger air of public life, even though that air was often tainted by impurities. No doubt, too, twenty years of unrest and controversy must have left their mark even on Milton. In one of the very few places[3] where he "abides our question," Shakespeare writes:

> "O! for my sake do you with Fortune chide,
> The guilty goddess of my harmful deeds,
> That did not better for my life provide,
> Than public means, which public manners breeds:
> Thence comes it that my name receives a brand;
> And almost thence my nature is subdu'd
> To what it works in, like the dyer's hand."

Milton's genius was subdued in this way. If we compare him, the Milton of the great epics and of *Samson Agonistes*, with Homer or Shakespeare—and none but the greatest can be his parallel—we find in him a certain want of humanity, a touch of narrowness. He lacks the large-heartedness, the genial, generous breadth of Shake-speare; the tolerant sympathy with his fellow men that even in *Troilus and Cressida* or *Timon of Athens* is there for those who have eyes wherewith to see it. Milton reflects many of the less gracious aspects of

---

[1] The italics are not Milton's.
[2] *Reason of Church Government*, P. W. II. 481.
[3] *Sonnet* CXI.

Puritanism, its intolerance, want of humour, one-sided intensity. He is stern and austere, and it seems natural to assume that this narrowness was to a great extent the price he paid for many years of ceaseless special pleading and dispute. The real misfortune of his life lay in the fact that he fell on evil, angry days when there was no place for moderate men. He had to be one of two things: either a controversialist or a student: there was no *via media.* Probably he chose aright; but we could wish that there had been no necessity to make the choice.

The last part of Milton's life, 1660—1674, passed quietly. At the age of fifty-two he was thrown back upon poetry, and could at length discharge his self-imposed obligation. *From the Restoration to Milton's death.* The early poems he had never regarded as a fulfilment of the debt due to his Creator; even when the fire of political strife burned at its hottest Milton never lost sight of the purpose which had been with him since his boyhood. The main difficulty lay in the selection of a suitable subject. He had weighed themes drawn from the Scriptures and others taken from the history of his own country. For a time he was evidently in- *His great work; the subject and treatment.* clined to choose the Arthurian story[1], the only cycle of events in British history or legend which seems to lend itself naturally to epic treatment. Had he done so we should have lost the *Idylls of the King.* The rough drafts of his projected schemes, now among the Milton

---

[1] This project is not mentioned among the schemes enumerated in the Trinity MSS. But cf. the *Epitaphium Damonis,* 162—178, and the poem *Mansus,* 80—84. See also *Comus,* 826—842, *Lycidas,* 160 (note). Among Milton's prose works was a *History of Britain,* written for the most part about 1649, but not printed till 1670. In it he used the materials collected for his abandoned epic on the story of King Arthur.

MSS. at Trinity College[1], shew that exactly ninety-nine possible themes occupied his thoughts from time to time; but even as early as 1641 the story of the lost Paradise began to assume prominence. Still, even when the subject was definitely chosen, the question of its treatment—dramatic or epic—remained. Milton contemplated the former. He even commenced work upon a drama of which Satan's address to the sun in the fourth book of *Paradise Lost*[2] formed the exordium. These lines were written about 1642. Milton recited them to his nephew Phillips at the time of their composition. Possibly, had Milton not been distracted and diverted from poetry by political and other interests, he might from 1642 onwards have continued this drama, and thus produced a dramatic masterpiece akin to *Samson Agonistes*. As things fell out, the scheme was dropped, and never taken up again. When he finally addressed himself to the composition of *Paradise Lost* he had decided in favour of the epic or narrative form.

Following Aubrey (from Aubrey and Phillips most of

Paradise Lost begun. our information concerning Milton is derived) we may assume that Milton began to write *Paradise Lost* about 1658. He worked continuously at the epic for some five years. It was finished in 1663, the year of his third[3] marriage. Two more years, however,

---

[1] They include the original drafts of *Arcades*, *Comus*, *Lycidas*, and some of the minor poems, together with Milton's notes on the design of the long poem he meditated composing, and other less important papers. The MSS. were presented to Trinity by a former member of the college, Sir Henry Newton Puckering, who died in 1700. It is not known how they originally came into his possession.

[2] Bk. IV. ll. 32 *et seq.*

[3] Milton's second marriage took place in the autumn of 1656, i.e. after he had become blind. His wife died in February, 1658. Cf. the *Sonnet*, "Methought I saw my late espoused

were spent in the necessary revision, and in 1665 Milton placed the completed poem in the hands of his friend Thomas Ellwood[1]. In 1667 *Paradise Lost* was issued from the press[2]. Milton received *The poem published.* £5. Before his death he was paid a second instalment, £5. Six editions of the poem had been published by the close of the century.

When Ellwood returned the MS. of *Paradise Lost* to Milton he remarked: "Thou hast said much here of *Paradise Lost*, but what hast thou to say of Paradise found?" Possibly we owe *Paradise Regained* to these chance words; or the poem, *Paradise Regained: Samson Agonistes.* forming as it does a natural pendant to its predecessor, may have been included in Milton's original design. In any case he must have commenced the second epic about the year 1665. *Samson Agonistes* appears to have been written a little later. The two poems were published together in 1671.

In giving this bare summary of facts it has not been

saint," the pathos of which is heightened by the fact that he had never seen her.

[1] Cf. the account given in Ellwood's *Autobiography:* "after some common discourses had passed between us, he called for a manuscript of his; which, being brought, he delivered to me, bidding me take it home with me and read it at my leisure, and, when I had so done, return it to him with my judgment thereupon. When I came home, and had set myself to read it, I found it was that excellent poem which he intituled *Paradise Lost.*"

[2] The delay was due to external circumstances. Milton had been forced by the Plague to leave London, settling for a time at Chalfont St Giles in Buckinghamshire, where Ellwood had taken a cottage for him. On his return to London, after "the sickness was over, and the city well cleansed," the Great Fire threw everything into disorder; and there was some little difficulty over the licensing of the poem. For these reasons the publication of *Paradise Lost* was delayed till the autumn of 1667 (Masson).

our purpose to offer any criticism upon the poems. It would take too much space to show why *Samson Agonistes* is in subject-matter the poet's threnody over the fallen form of Puritanism, and in style the most perfectly classical poem in English literature ; or again, why some great writers (among them Coleridge and Wordsworth) have pronounced *Paradise Regained* to be in point of artistic execution the most consummate of Milton's works—a judgment which would have pleased the author himself since, according to Phillips, he could never endure to hear *Paradise Regained* "censured to be much inferior to *Paradise Lost.*" The latter speaks for itself in the rolling splendour of those harmonies which Tennyson has celebrated and alone in his time equalled.

In 1673 Milton brought out a reprint of the 1645 *Close of* edition of his *Poems*, adding most of the *Milton's life.* sonnets[1] written in the interval. The last four years of his life were devoted to prose works of no

---

[1] The number of Milton's sonnets is twenty-three (if we exclude the piece on "The New Forcers of Conscience"), five of which were written in Italian, probably during the time of his travels in Italy, 1638—9. Ten sonnets were printed in the edition of 1645, the last of them being that entitled (from the *Cambridge* MS.) "To the Lady Margaret Ley." The remaining thirteen were composed between 1645 and 1658. The concluding sonnet, therefore (to the memory of Milton's second wife), immediately preceded his commencement of *Paradise Lost.* Four of these poems (XV. XVI. XVII. XXII.) could not, on account of their political tone, be included in the edition of 1673. They were first published by Edward Phillips at the end of his memoir of Milton, 1694. The sonnet on the "Massacre in Piedmont" is usually considered the finest of the collection, of which the late Rector of Lincoln College edited a well-known edition, 1883. The sonnet inscribed with a diamond on a window pane in the cottage at Chalfont where the poet stayed in 1665 is (in the judgment of a good critic) Miltonic, if not Milton's (Garnett's *Life of Milton*, p. 175).

particular interest to us[1]. He continued to live in London. His third marriage had proved happy, and he enjoyed something of the renown which was rightly his. Various well-known men used to visit him—notably Dryden[2], who on one of his visits asked and received permission to dramatise *Paradise Lost*.

Milton died in 1674, November 8th. He was buried in St Giles's Church, Cripplegate. When we think of him we have to think of a man who *His death.* lived a life of very singular purity and devotion to duty ; who for what he conceived to be his country's good sacrificed—and no one can well estimate the sacrifice— during twenty years the aim that was nearest to his heart and best suited to his genius ; who, however, eventually realised his desire of writing a great work *in gloriam Dei.*

[1] The treatise on *Christian Doctrine* is valuable as throwing much light on the theological views expressed in the two epic poems and *Samson Agonistes.*

[2] The lines by Dryden which were printed beneath the portrait of Milton in Tonson's folio edition of *Paradise Lost* published in 1688 are too familiar to need quotation ; but it is worth noting that the younger poet had in Milton's lifetime described the great epic as "one of the most noble, and most sublime poems which either this age or nation has produced" (prefatory essay to *The State of Innocence*, 1674). Further, tradition assigned to Dryden (a Roman Catholic and a Royalist) the remark, "this fellow (Milton) cuts us all out and the ancients too."

COMUS.

Comus was probably written in the spring of 1634. There can be no doubt that its composition was due to Milton's intimate friend Henry Lawes, the musician. Among Lawes's pupils were the family of the Earl of

Why written, and when.

Bridgewater, son-in-law of the Countess of Derby, in whose honour *Arcades* was written. In July 1631 the Earl of Bridgewater was made Lord-Lieutenant of the counties on the Welsh border and of North and South Wales—a viceregal post similar to the Lord-Lieutenancy of Ireland. For some reason the Earl's formal entry on his duties was delayed till the autumn of 1634. To celebrate the event great festivities were held at his official residence, Ludlow Castle. The first performance of *Comus* was part of these festivities. It took place on Michaelmas night, 1634. Doubtless Lawes, as music-master to the Earl's family, and as a practised writer of Masque-music, had been asked to undertake the provision of an entertainment suitable to the occasion, and had applied to Milton for help. With the Puritan Milton of later years, who in *Paradise Lost*, IV. 764, decried "mixed dance or wanton masque," the petition would have fared ill. But at this time there could be nothing distasteful in it. Milton showed himself in *L'Allegro* friendly to the stage, admitting "masque and antique pageantry" among the legitimate delights that Mirth might offer. Further, there was the desire to do a service to his friend Lawes. Milton accepted the commission, and *Comus* was the outcome.

Date of "Comus."

Probably he wrote the piece early in 1634. It had to be ready by the autumn; and time would be required for the setting of the music, and for all the preparations incidental to the representation of an unusually long Masque. The spring therefore of 1634 may be received with some confidence as the date of the composition of *Comus*.

Whether the play was successful at its representation we do not know. Many of Lawes's friends evidently appreciated it. Some were present in the Hall at Ludlow Castle on that September evening; others, perhaps, heard the songs afterwards sung by Lawes himself or his pupils. They realised that there was in England a poet of rare promise and exquisite performance. Copies of *Comus* were asked for; it became "much desired[1]." At last, to save himself the trouble of making these transcripts, Lawes published an edition of *Comus*, probably from the MS. which had been used as the acting-version. This, the first edition of *Comus*, was issued in 1637. The title-page describes the poem as "A Maske presented at Ludlow Castle, 1634, *The first edition of "Comus."* on Michaelmasse Night, before the Right Honourable John, Earle of Bridgewater, Viscount Brackley, Lord President of Wales, and one of his Majestie's most honourable Privy Counsell.

> ' *Eheu quid volui misero mihi! floribus Austrum Perditus—*' "

It will be observed that Milton's name is omitted. The motto, however (from Vergil, *Eclogue*, II. 58, 59), shows that his consent to the publication had been obtained: "Alas! what have I been about in my folly! On my flowers I have let in the sirocco (i.e. the hot south-east wind), infatuate as I am." The last words imply that Milton had some doubt as to the expediency of printing the volume. Had Lawes issued the imprint against the wishes of Milton, the motto chosen would have been pointless. It reminds us of the reluctance to break his silence "before the mellowing year" which he expressed at the beginning of *Lycidas* in that same year,

[1] See p. 3.

1637. That at least one competent and discerning critic was ready to welcome the new voice in English verse we may judge from Sir Henry Wotton's complimentary letter to Milton[1].

Editions of Milton's minor poems appeared in 1645
Later editions of "Comus."   and 1673. *Comus*, of course, was printed in each. In neither, however, did he describe the poem by the name it has long borne. The title in the 1645 edition reads thus: "A Mask of the Same Author, Presented at Ludlow Castle, 1634, before the Earl of Bridgewater, then President of Wales: Anno Dom. 1645." The title of the later edition is almost identical. A more definite designation being desirable, the Masque was named *Comus* after its chief character.

The basis of the text of *Comus* is supplied by
The Text.   the three above-mentioned editions—that of Lawes, 1637, and those of Milton, 1645 and 1673. Milton's original draft of the poem is among the MSS.[2] at Cambridge; and the Bridgewater manuscript, supposed to be the stage-copy from which the actors learned their parts, and believed to be in Lawes's handwriting, also survives. All the differences between these five authorities—on the whole, not inconsiderable differences—we have not attempted to record. A careful comparison of them was given by Todd, and it is instructive to note the unerring instinct with which Milton, like Tennyson, always corrected his work for the better. Perhaps the last of the editions published during Milton's life has the most weight. It gives us *Comus*, not as the Masque originally left Milton's hands—for that we must turn to the Cambridge MS.—but in the finally revised form which he wished it to assume. There is a single passage where one is fain to believe that the Cambridge manuscript is right, and the printed copies

[1] See p. 4.
[2] *i.e.* the Milton MSS. at Trinity College; see p. xxii.

wrong. This is line 553. Milton's blindness necessarily introduces a slight uncertainty as to the text of his poems published in the latter part of his life.

Such, in brief, is the external history of *Comus*. Something must be said about the poem itself—the sources from which Milton drew, the undercurrent of idea that runs throughout, the dramatic value of the Masque, its ethical and literary qualities.

In lines 43—45 the Attendant Spirit says:

> "I will tell you now
> What never yet was heard in tale or song,
> From old or modern bard, in hall or bower."

The sources of "Comus."

This claim to absolute originality must not be pressed. Milton was indebted in *Comus*, in some measure, to previous writers. We shall best be able to estimate the debt if we split up the Masque into its chief component parts.

There is (1) the main story: that of the sister lost in a wood, entrapped by a magician, and rescued by her brothers; with the attendant incidents. This Milton owed, it is almost certain, to the *Old Wives' Tale* (1595) of

Milton's debt to George Peele (1558—1595).

George Peele, the Elizabethan poet (1558—1598). Warton summarised thus the points of contact between *Comus* and the *Old Wives' Tale:* "This curious piece (i.e. Peele's play) exhibits, among other parallel incidents, two Brothers wandering in quest of their Sister, whom an Enchanter had imprisoned. This magician had learned his art from his mother Meroe, as Comus had been instructed by his mother Circe. The Brothers call out the Lady's name, and Echo replies[1]. The Enchanter had given her a potion which suspends the power of reason, and superinduces oblivion of herself. The Brothers afterwards meet with an Old Man, who is also skilled in magic; and by listening to his soothsayings,

---

[1] In *Comus* it is the Lady who invokes the Echo.

they recover their lost Sister. But not till the Enchanter's wreath has been torn from his head, his sword wrested from his hand, a glass broken, and a light extinguished."

Warton's abstract of the *Old Wives' Tale* somewhat accentuates the resemblance. It does not strike us quite so forcibly when we read Peele's work. Still the similarity is there, and Milton's indebtedness to Peele is universally admitted.

The popular tradition, still extant, as to the genesis of

The tradi-tional account of the origin of "Comus."

Comus must also be mentioned. This was to the effect that the young Lady Alice Egerton and her two brothers, Viscount Brackley and Mr Thomas Egerton, were actually overtaken by nightfall in Haywood Forest, near Ludlow : they were returning to the castle from a visit to their relatives, the Egertons, in Herefordshire, and the sister was separated from her brothers. If this ever took place and news of it reached Milton's ears, then he simply dramatised the episode ; though part of his debt to Peele, viz. the intro-duction of the magician, would still remain. But it seems more probable that the legend, which cannot be traced further back than the last century, grew out of the Masque.

(2) The chief character of the piece, Comus, introduces

The cha-racter of Comus, the magician.

another element in the story. He is in all essentials the creation of Milton. In classical Greek κῶμος signifies 'revel' or 'revelling-band.' The word κῶμος was specially used of the band of revellers[1] at the vintage festivals held in honour of Dionysus the god of wine (=the Roman god Bacchus). Thence naturally arose the personification Comus, i.e. revelling or sensual pleasure regarded as a

---

[1] The Cambridge MS of *Comus* has the stage-direction "intrant κωμάζοντες" ('they enter in revelling fashion') at line 93. And in the list of possible subjects of Milton's great poem is the entry "*Comazontes*, or The Benjaminites, or The Rioters," with references to *Judges* xix, xx, xxi.

kind of deity; but this is a post-classical conception, known only to later mythology. Apparently this deity Comus is first mentioned by the Greek writer Philostratus the elder, who lived in the third century A.D. and wrote a book on paintings, under the title "Likenesses, Portraits" (*Imagines*). Philostratus describes a fresco in which Comus is represented as a youth ruddy with wine, but the account is too slight to have been of much service to Milton, even if he was familiar with it. More definite is the picture drawn by Ben Jonson in the Masque of *Pleasure Reconciled to Virtue* (1619). Comus is a character in that Masque and described as

> "The founder of taste
> For fresh meats, or powdered, or pickle, or paste;
> Devourer of boiled, baked, roasted or sod;
> An emptier of cups."

Obviously this sordid power of dull, "lust-dieted" appetite has not very much in common with Milton's blithe, caressing personification of pleasure, so fatal because outwardly so beautiful; though I do not doubt that Milton knew Ben Jonson's Masque.

There is also a certain Latin play which may have given suggestions and which derives from its title deserves to be mentioned. It was called *Comus*. It was written by a Dutchman, *The Latin Play, "Comus."* Hendrik van der Putten (better known under the name of Erycius Puteanus), sometime professor at Louvain. First printed in 1608, his *Comus* was reissued at Oxford in 1634, a remarkable coincidence. The Comus of Puteanus is a much subtler embodiment of sensuality than the cup-quaffing deity of Ben Jonson; he approximates more to the graceful reveller and enticing magician of Milton, and I should be loath to acquit Milton of all indebtedness to Puteanus. I think that he must have gone through the Latin piece, picking out from the worthless slag an occasional atom of genuine ore.

The extremely appropriate parentage which is assigned to Comus (46—58) was Milton's own invention. It was partly suggested, no doubt, by the association of the word κῶμος with Dionysus (Bacchus). Milton's purpose in making Comus the son of Circe and inheritor of her magic powers was to bring out the enticing aspect of sensual pleasure, which seeks to cast its beguiling spells upon men.

(3) The third strand in the material out of which

Milton's use of the legend of Circe. *Comus* is woven is the Circe-myth. In describing the supernatural powers of Comus Milton transfers to the wizard the classical attributes of his mother Circe. Like Vergil and Ovid before him, he lays the *Odyssey* under large contribution : so had Spenser in his account of the enchantress Acrasia in *The Faerie Queene*, II. 12, 55 *et seq.* Browne, too, had made the adventure of Odysseus and his crew at the island of Circe the theme of *The Inner Temple Masque* (1614). Probably each account—certainly Spenser's—was known to Milton, and may have exercised an unconscious influence upon him, *e.g.* in the turn of a phrase or addition of a descriptive detail. Going over the same ground as other writers with whom he is in any degree familiar, a poet can scarcely escape being influenced in some way, even though he is quite unaware of it.

(4) There remains the legend of the river-goddess

The Story of Sabrina. Milton's indebtedness to Fletcher. Sabrina, whose intervention frees the imprisoned lady and brings the Masque to a happy close. The source of this legend, which had been handled by other poets, was the *History* of Geoffrey of Monmouth[1]. In this important part of *Comus* the influence of Fletcher's *Faithful Shepherdess* is unmistakeable. This beautiful pastoral was composed before 1625. It had been acted as a Court-drama, and representations were given in the

[1] See p. 133

London theatres in 1633 and 1634. The motive of the play is identical with that of *Comus*, viz. the strength of purity; and in Fletcher's heroine must be recognised an elder sister of Milton's Sabrina. Speaking briefly we may say that the last two hundred lines of *Comus*—the disenchantment scene—betray in the conception of the nymph Sabrina, in the incidents, and the lyric movement, the spell which Fletcher's genius exercised on Milton. Milton chose the story of the goddess who swayed the Severn stream in compliment to his audience. It suited the scene and the setting of his Masque; and his treatment of the theme reflects, in no servile spirit of imitation, the graceful example of the poet with whom the name of Shakespeare himself is linked in more than one work.

It is not doing Milton any real service to ignore or deny his indebtedness to these various sources. Absolute, unqualified originality is practically impossible. Literature is a series of echoes, and one of the tests of genius is to take inferior work and tune it to finer issues. Has the artist breathed fresh suggestion into things old? has he added things new? If we can answer 'yes' to each of these questions, his record is clear. We must indeed always try to get a clear idea wherein lies the greatness of a work, what are the qualities that make it immortal. In *Comus* those qualities, surely, are the exquisite music, especially of the lyric portions, the rapt elevation of thought and tone, the distinction of style. These gifts are a poet's own. He does not obtain them from 'sources,' search he never so carefully. And they constitute the 'originality' that is essential.

It is manifestly unfair to judge any work by tests which do not properly apply to it: we must not condemn a thing for not being what it does not profess to be—a truism which *"Comus" to be judged as a Masque.* criticism often ignores. So it is beside the mark to say that *Comus* is "deficient as a drama." It does not profess to be a "drama" in the sense that *The Merchant of Venice* or *Hamlet* is. It is a " Masque." Now in a Masque we are not to look for the qualities which are indispensable to an ordinary drama, such as probability of story and logical development of dramatic motive, propriety of construction, studied and consistent character-drawing[1]. These things lie outside the province of the Masque-writer, whose fancy plays unfettered in a land where truth and realism seldom set foot. Consequently *Comus* should not be contrasted with works that belong to a different sphere of art. To estimate its merits aright we should study what Ben Jonson and Fletcher, the ablest of professional Masque-writers, have left us of a like description. We must accord Milton the licence which the composers of such pieces habitually claimed, and test *Comus* by the elementary standard of dramatic propriety recognised in these entertainments. Judged so, it has no cause to fear the objection that its story lacks probability or its construction violates rule.

On the other hand, there is one objection to *Comus* which we cannot gainsay: as a Masque designed for representation it is over-weighted with the moralising element. Magnificent in itself and intensely interesting as a revelation of Milton's character and of his relation towards the peculiar religious and social conditions of his age, this lofty strain of moralising is out of place in a Masque. It fits neither the occasion nor the speakers[2]. You cannot but feel that Milton uses the long speeches of the Lady and the Elder Brother to expound views which he holds especially sacred. All great art teaches, but the teaching is indirect. In *Comus* the didactic purpose is patent; nay, obtrudes. It hampers the movement of the piece, checks the natural

Its moralising.

---

[1] In *Comus* the absence of names for all the characters except Comus should prepare us for the slightness of the characterisation.

[2] Hence the significant omissions, made doubtless by Lawes, at the original performance. See notes on 195—225, 737—755. One passage, 779—806, was an addition.

progress of the story; and worse, it strikes a note alien to the genius of the fanciful Masque and all its festive associations. But this demerit is characteristic of the poet. Milton's one defect, what more than aught else marks him Shakespeare's inferior, is lack of humour. A sense of humour means a keen sense of the incongruous; and a writer with half Milton's genius but more of that sense would have shunned the incongruous element which mars *Comus* as a Masque while increasing its power and beauty as a poem. It is, therefore, as a poem that the piece should be regarded, and the long speeches "must be read as majestic soliloquies" (Macaulay).

This didactic element reveals Milton, and that at a point of special interest in his career. It teaches the doctrine nearest to his heart, *"The Miltonic idea" embodied in "Comus."* namely, sobriety of life. There was nothing for which Milton cared more than this. An atmosphere of rare purity breathes in his works. He shows an extraordinarily nice sense of whatsoever things are fair and good report. There is in him a strong vein of asceticism, and he praises more than once the "cloistered virtue" of abstinence. As a youth he described thus, in a strain of classical allusion, the obligations of those who would touch the highest reaches of poetic art:

"But they, who demi-gods and heroes praise,
  And feats performed in Jove's more youthful days,
  Who now the counsels of high heaven explore,
  Now shades that echo the Cerberean roar,
  Simply let these, like him of Samos, live,
  Let herbs to them a bloodless banquet give;
  In beechen goblets let their beverage shine,
  Cool from the crystal spring their sober wine.
  Their youth should pass in innocence secure
  From stain licentious, and in manners pure,
  Pure as the priest, when robed in white he stands,
  The fresh lustration ready in his hands.

> Thus Linus lived, and thus, as poets write,
> Tiresias, wiser for his loss of sight.
> Thus exiled Chalcas, thus the bard of Thrace,
> Melodious tamer of the savage race.
> Thus trained by temperance, Homer led of yore
> His chief of Ithaca from shore to shore.
> For these are sacred bards, and from above
> Drink large infusions from the mind of Jove[1]."

That was his youthful ideal : his works and all that we know of his life show that it was his practice. Professor Masson well sums up the matter in the statement that "the sublime notion and high mystery" of a disciplined life is "*the* Miltonic idea." Nowhere is it more conspicuous than in this Masque.

Under any circumstances the theme would have kindled

The Puritans and the Cavaliers. his muse to eloquence. But now in the year 1634, when the people were slowly separating into hostile camps, the truth was of more than personal import: it had become vitalised with a tragic national intensity. Each day the conflict between the gloom and ungraciousness of Puritanism and the pleasure-seeking carelessness of the Cavalier world grew keener. Extremes produce extremes : for one part of the nation life meant pleasure : the other identified pleasure with sin. When *Comus* was written Milton stood between the two armies. His Puritanism was tempered by Renaissance culture. The life of ideal happiness as pictured in *L'Allegro* is one into which enter all the influences of culture and nature that bring in their train "the joy in widest commonalty spread ;" the cheerfulness which should be synonymous with Life, and to which Art should minister. And when in *Il Penseroso* Milton celebrates divinest Melancholy, she is not the bitter power whom Dante punished with the pains of Purgatory ; rather, she has something of the kindliness

---

[1] From the sixth of the Latin *Elegies*, Cowper's translation.

that Shakespeare attributes to his goddess Adversity, whose uses are sweet, and of whom it was happily said that she must be a fourth Grace, less known than the classic Three, but still their sister.

These poems, *L'Allegro, Il Penseroso,* and *Comus,* belong to the non-political period in Milton's life. The bare fact that he wrote the last showed that he had not yet gone over to help the party whose unreasoning hatred of all amusement had flashed out in Prynne's *Histrio-mastix*[1] (1633). As Green says, "the historic interest of *Comus* lies in its forming part of a protest made by the more cultured Puritans against the gloomier bigotry which persecution was fostering in the party at large." On the other hand, the whole tone of *Comus* was opposed to the spirit of the Cavaliers. It sternly rebuked intemperance. The revel-god personified the worst elements of Court-life. In his overthrow Milton allegorically foreshadowed the downfall of those who led that life; just as in *Lycidas,* under the guise of pastoral symbolism, he predicted the ruin of the "corrupted Clergie," and at the end of his life lamented the crash of Puritanism through the mouth of Samson Agonistes. Two hundred and fifty years ago therefore *Comus* was terribly real as a warning against the danger upon which the ship of national life was drifting. But the theme is true yesterday, to-day, and for ever; and the art with which it is enforced remains undimmed, the wisdom unfading.

Johnson had fault to find with the songs in *Comus.* He considered them "harsh," and "not very musical." This was the most curious feature of his strange, grudging criticism of

The lyrical parts of "Comus."

---

[1] Prynne often refers to Masques, and always in terms of scorn; *e.g.* on page 783 of the *Histriomastix,* "Stage-players, Mûmeries, Masques, and such like heathenish practises," 1633 ed.

the Masque, since the superlative excellence of Milton's lyrics has never been a matter of dispute. In them Milton achieves a style of quintessential beauty, reminding us with Wordsworth that poetry is primarily a matter of inspiration, and proving, like Gray, that it must also be a matter of art. Richness of imagery, epithets that (in Macaulay's words) supply "a text for a canto," single phrases that for their curious felicity are, as Archbishop Trench said, "poems in miniature," evanescent touches that recall to the classical reader the old and happy, far-off things of Athens and Rome—these qualities, that belong mainly to art, are held together and heightened by a perfect genuineness of emotion which is the outcome of sheer inspiration. Above all, Milton gives us what we require most in lyric verse—true melody, and those who are deaf to these sphere-born notes, who find the "numbers" of *Comus* unpleasing, must be left to their displeasure.

Most of us will prefer Mr Saintsbury's verdict: "It is impossible to single out passages, for the whole is golden. The entering address of Comus, the song 'Sweet Echo,' the descriptive speech of the Spirit, and the magnificent eulogy of the 'sun-clad power of chastity,' would be the most beautiful things where all is beautiful, if the unapproachable 'Sabrina fair' did not come later, and were not sustained before and after, for nearly two hundred lines of pure nectar."

It was a happy inspiration which reserved the rhymed parts mainly for the close, where they form a kind of lyric *cadenza* on which the Masque closes. After bearing the heat and burden of the piece, after enforcing with all the power of his eloquence and righteous enthusiasm the moral which *Comus* illustrates, Milton turned to his muse and bade her touch a lighter, festive note. The philosophic strain was dropped: the poet of *L'Allegro* reasserted himself; and *Comus* came to an end with Lawes's music ringing through the Hall.

The stage-history of *Comus* is very slight. The representation at Ludlow appears to be the only one that took place in the seventeenth century. It is interesting to note that part *Stage-history.* at least of the music written by Lawes for the original performance survives, viz. the five numbers, "From the heavens," "Sweet Echo," "Sabrina fair," "Back Shepherds" and "Now my task." In the last century most of Milton's minor poems were made to supply *libretti* for contemporary musicians. Handel set *L'Allegro* and *Il Penseroso* (1740) to music, and afterwards (1742) made *Samson Agonistes* the basis of his Oratorio. *Comus*, or rather an adaptation of it, fell to the skilful hands of Dr Arne, the composer to whom we owe some of the best known settings of Shakespeare's songs. The adaptation of the Masque was made by the Rev. John Dalton, afterwards Canon of Worcester. He altered it beyond recognition, dividing it into three acts, redistributing the speeches, introducing fresh characters (among them Lycidas) and scenes, and interpolating songs of his own composition. The most curious change occurs in Act III., which commences with twenty-six lines ("But come, thou goddess," line 11) taken from *L'Allegro*, the invocation to Mirth being followed by the appearance on the scene of Euphrosyne.

This stage-version was produced at Drury Lane theatre in 1738, and was frequently acted and several times printed. On the title-page of the first imprint (1738) are the words "never presented but on Michaelmas Day, 1634."

Geneste in his *Annals of the Stage* mentions later stage-versions with Arne's music, notably one for which Sir Henry Bishop wrote additional airs. Altogether *Comus* seems to have had some vogue on the stage in a quasi-operatic form. The last notable rendering of the Masque was that produced by Macready, who himself played the part of the magician.

METRICAL FEATURES OF THE POEM.

To those who desire more insight into the poetic Art of Milton it may be helpful to note a few important points of metre[1]. First as to the blank verse of *Comus*. The typical blank verse is a line of ten syllables forming five feet in which the stresses or accents fall on the even syllables. These feet are commonly termed "iambic[2]," and the rhythm of a line composed of iambic feet is a "rising" rhythm. Here is a typical blank verse from *Comus* (line 30):

The typical blank verse.

"And áll this tráct that frónts the fálling sún."

Blank verse prior to Marlowe, the great Elizabethan dramatist whose work influenced Shakespeare, was modelled strictly on this type. Further, this early blank verse was what is termed "end-stopt": that is to say, there was almost always *some* pause, however slight, in the sense, and consequently in the rhythm, at the close of each line; while the couplet was normally the limit of the sense. As an example of "end-stopt" verse look at *Comus*, 73—77:

"And they, so perfect is their misery,
Not once perceive their foul disfigurement,
But boast themselves more comely than before,
And all their friends and native home forget,
To roll with pleasure in a sensual sty."

[1] An authoritative work is Mr Bridges's book *Milton's Prosody*, on which I have drawn.

[2] An iambus in Greek prosody is a foot of two syllables, short + long, thus $\smile$ $-$. Roughly speaking, stress or accent is the equivalent in English prosody for the "quantity" of classical prosody; i.e. a stressed syllable (´) corresponds with the long syllable (–) of classical verse, and an unstressed syllable with the short ($\smile$). In "scanning" a passage it is better always to use the term "stress" or "accent" than "long syllable," and the symbol ´, not $-$.

If the whole poem were written in verse of this kind the effect, obviously, would be intolerably monotonous. Blank verse before Marlowe *was* intolerably monotonous, and his great service to metre, carried further by Shakespeare, was to introduce variations into the existing type of the blank decasyllabic measure. In fact, analysis of the blank verse of any writer really resolves itself into a study of his modifications of the purely "iambic," "end-stopt" type.

The four chief variations employed by Milton[1] in *Comus* are these :

Milton's chief variations.

(1) His use of the "overflow" of the sense from one line to another; what the French call "*enjambement*."

The "overflow."

Put simply, this only means that he makes the sense and rhythm run on from one line to another. A large proportion of his blank verse is "unstopt," not "end-stopt." Take *Comus*, 1—4 :

> " Before the starry threshold of Jove's court
> My mansion is, where those immortal shapes
> Of bright aerial spirits live insphered
> In regions mild of calm and serene air."

In those lines there is no pause of sense and consequently none of rhythm at the end of either of lines 1—3 : sense and rhythm run on.

Now "unstopt" verse escapes one of the dangers of blank verse : the danger of being stiff and formal, and hampering the sense, as in the early days of the metre, through arrangement in single lines or couplets. But it incurs another danger : it may be loose and formless through want of clearly marked pauses, balance of the parts, and rhythmic cadences—the qualities which should compensate for the absence of rhyme. Blank verse therefore of the "unstopt" type in which the paragraph is the unit, not the single line or couplet, needs an exquisite

---

[1] Not necessarily peculiar to him.

sense of sound, and of sound harmonised in a complex, elaborate scheme. And this sense was Milton's great gift. Hence his blank verse unites the two qualities so difficult to reconcile, yet essential, namely freedom and form: the freedom which allows an easy, natural expression of the sense and a variety of rhythm that echoes all its shifting inflections; and the form which comes from consummate mastery of pause, balance and cadence. Thus much as to the arrangement of his lines: now as to their internal formation.

(2) The second great feature of his blank verse is the use of "extrametrical" syllables. Briefly, he sometimes has eleven or even twelve syllables instead of ten in a line. The extra syllable may come (*a*) at the end of the line, (*b*) about the middle after some pause, or (*c*) in both places. Here are examples (211, 67, 617):

"Extra-metrical" syllables.

(*a*) "The virtuous mind, that ever walks attend(ed)."

(*b*) "To quench the drouth of Phœ(bus); which as they taste."

(*c*) "As to make this rela(tion)? Cáre and útmost (shifts)."

Far the commonest of these variations from the typical decasyllabic line is (*a*). It is a great feature of the verse of *Comus* and *Samson Agonistes*. The proportion of such lines as (*a*) is said to be 1 in 9 in *Comus*, 1 in 6 in *Samson Agonistes*. In *Paradise Lost*, on the other hand, this kind of verse is rare. This is the one great difference between Milton's early and late blank verse, and the reason for it is clear. The extra syllable at the end of the line tends to make the rhythm run on into the next line, and therefore gives a rapid movement suitable to the spoken verse of the stage. It characterises thus the dramatic and lyrical pieces, whilst epic narrative like *Paradise Lost* demands a statelier, slower movement.

This extrametrical syllable at the end of a line is commonly called the "double" or "feminine" ending.

Note that it is of two kinds—where the last syllable would naturally bear a stress or accent, and where it would not.

Thus contrast 265

"And she shall be my queen. Hail, foreign wón(dĕr)"

with 633

"Bore a bright golden flower, but not in thís (sóil)."

Illustrations of (b) are lines 302, 415, 599, 662, 842.

The other variation (c) is also illustrated, I think, by line 407.

(3) Another feature is "inversion of rhythm," i.e. the substitution of "falling" rhythm for "rising" by use of a trochee in place of an iambus, these feet being exact opposites. A trochee is admitted into any of the first four feet of a line. Compare

"Inversion of rhythm."

(a) "Stríve to | keep up a frail and feverish being" (8);

(b) "Be well | stóck'd with | as fair a herd as grazed" (152);

(c) "But to my task. | Néptune | besides the sway" (18);

(d) "Benighted in these woods. | Nów to | my charms" (150).

Observe that inversion generally gives some emphasis to the word. Much the commonest inversion is that of the first foot. Indeed, this use of an initial trochee is one of the most characteristic points in Milton's verse. Among many examples take lines 39 ("thréats the"), 46 ("Bácchus"), 47 ("crúsh'd the"), 49 ("cóasting"), with 60, 79, 80, 90, 147, 162, 163, 190 etc. In 145 there are two trochees ("bréak off, bréak off"); but I have not observed a similar instance. The trochee is a swift foot, and you will see that in several of the examples just given the sense refers to motion of some sort.

(4) The last point is the use of weak stresses. Sometimes there are less than five strong stresses in a line. This occurs most often where there is a preposition, and is com-

"Weak Stresses."

monest in the first and fourth feet. It gives, by way of
compensation, a peculiar heaviness, as of two[1] stressed
syllables, to the following foot. Compare these instances:

(a) " Before | the star|ry thres|hold òf | Jove's court" (1) ;

(b) "With thè | rank va|pours of this sin-worn mould " (17) ;

(c) " Ere mor|row wake, | or thè | low-roost|ed lark" (317) ;

(d) "Stépped, as | they said, | to thè | next thick|et side" (185).

Observe that the variations (2), (3) and (4) may be used
in combination, e.g. we find all three in line 49

"Coásting | the Týr|rhene shóre | as thè | winds líst(ed),"

and in 617

" As tò | make thís | relá(tion)? | Cáre and | útmost (shifts) " ;

and (3) and (4) in line 185 (quoted just above).

The lyrics of *Comus* are simple in structure, cast for

Metre of the lyrics. the most part in the octosyllabic measure, in
"rising" rhythm, much used by Ben Jonson
and easily set as musical recitative. They
show that Milton exercised very freely the right of using im-

Imperfect rhyme. perfect rhymes. As proof of this Professor
Masson aptly refers to the Echo Song. It has
fourteen lines, with four consecutive pairs of
irregular rhyme ; and it is none the less wholly beautiful.

Milton varies the eight-syllabled measure (1) by an

Variations in the octo-syllabic mea-sure. extra syllable at the end of the line, (2) by
lines of only seven syllables in "falling,"
i.e. trochaic rhythm, with an extra syllable,
stressed, at the end, (3) by occasional decasyllabic rhymed couplets.

For (1) compare 999

"Where young Adonis oft repo(ses) ";

[1] *i.e.* forming a spondaic foot, the classical spondee being
two long syllables (– –).

and for (2), which is by far the most important modification, cf. the following lines :

> "The stár | that bíds | the shép|herd fóld
> Nów the | tóp of | heáv'n doth | hóld;
> And the | gílded | cár of | dáy
> His glów|ing áx|le dóth | alláy."

For (3) see 115, 116, 129–132.

Then, it must be remembered that in all scansion of English poetry two things play a great part, viz. "contraction" and "elision."

"Contractions" may be divided into (1) the abbreviations of everyday speech, "such as the *Contractions.* perfect tenses and participles in *ed*, which Milton often writes *t*";

and (2) those of poetical usage, such as the *en=n* of the perfect participle, e.g. 'fall'n,' 'chos'n,' 'giv'n'; and *est='st* in the 2nd person singular of verbs, e.g. 'think'st,' 'saw'st,' 'gav'st.'

By "elision" one means "slurring" a letter or syllable so that it scarcely sounds at all, and metrically *Elision.* does not count. The (1) main principle of elision is that an "open" vowel, i.e. a vowel preceding a vowel, may be "slurred." The commonest instance is with the definite article. Compare line 11

"Amongst th(e) enthroned gods on sainted seats."

So with words like 'mans(i)on,' 'aer(i)al,' 'reg(i)on,' 'ambros(i)al,' 'imper(i)al,' 'var(i)ous,'—all in the first 30 lines of *Comus*. Also, (2) this principle of elision applies to an unstressed vowel preceding *r* or *n* or *l* in words like 'fev'rish,' 'ev'ry,' 'sev'ral,' 'wand'ring,' 'grov'lling,' 'om'nous,' 'count'nance,' 'advent'rous'; see *Comus*, 8, 19, 25, 39, 61, 68, 79. Many of the elisions roughly grouped under the headings (1) and (2) are such as we use in common speech.

Finally, some allowance must be made for the different

accentuation of some words[1] in Elizabethan and modern English.

[1] See *aspect* in the Glossary.

COMUS.

"A MASQUE PRESENTED AT LUDLOW CASTLE, 1634."

DEDICATION[1] OF THE ANONYMOUS EDITION OF 1637.

" To the Right Honourable John, Lord Brackley, son and heir-apparent to the Earl of Bridgewater etc."

"My Lord,

   This Poem, which received its first occasion of birth from yourself and others of your noble family, and much honour from your own person in the performance, now returns again to make a final dedication of itself to you. Although not openly acknowledged by the Author, yet it is a legitimate offspring, so lovely and so much desired that the often copying of it hath tired my pen to give my several friends satisfaction, and brought me to a necessity of producing it to the public view, and now to offer it up, in all rightful devotion, to those fair hopes and rare endowments of your much-promising youth, which give a full assurance to all that know you of a future excellence. Live, sweet Lord, to be the honour of your name ; and receive this as your own from the hands of him who hath by many favours been long obliged to your most honoured Parents, and, as in this representation your attendant *Thyrsis*, so now in all real expression

    Your most faithful and most humble Servant,

       H. LAWES."

---

[1] Reprinted in the edition of 1645 : omitted in that of 1673.

"The Copy[1] *of a Letter written by Sir Henry Wotton to the
Author upon the following Poem."*

"From the College, this 13 of April, 1638.

Sir,

It was a special favour when you lately bestowed
upon me here the first taste of your acquaintance, though no
longer than to make me know that I wanted more time to value
it and to enjoy it rightly; and, in truth, if I then could have
imagined your farther stay in these parts, which I understood
afterwards by Mr H., I would have been bold, in our vulgar
phrase, to mend my draught (for you left me with an extreme
thirst), and to have begged your conversation again, jointly with
your said learned friend, over a poor meal or two, that we
might have banded together some good Authors of the ancient
time; among which I observed you to have been familiar.

Since your going, you have charged me with new obligations, both for a very kind letter from you dated the 6th of this
month, and for a dainty piece of entertainment which came
therewith. Wherein I should much commend the tragical part,
if the lyrical did not ravish me with a certain Doric delicacy
in your Songs and Odes, whereunto I must plainly confess to
have seen yet nothing parallel in our language: *Ipsa mollities*.
But I must not omit to tell you that I now only owe you thanks
for intimating unto me (how modestly soever) the true artificer.
For the work itself I had viewed some good while before with
singular delight; having received it from our common friend
Mr R., in the very close of the late R.'s Poems, printed at
Oxford: whereunto it was added (as I now suppose) that the
accessory might help out the principal, according to the art of
Stationers, and to leave the reader *con la bocca dolce*.

Now, Sir, concerning your travels; wherein I may challenge
a little more privilege of discourse with you. I suppose you
will not blanch Paris in your way: therefore I have been bold
to trouble you with a few lines to Mr M. B., whom you shall

[1] Omitted in the reprint of 1673, this letter was given in the
edition of 1645.

easily find attending the young Lord S. as his governor; and you may surely receive from him good directions for the shaping of your farther journey into Italy where he did reside, by my choice, some time for the King, after mine own recess from Venice.

I should think that your best line will be through the whole length of France to Marseilles, and thence by sea to Genoa; whence the passage into Tuscany is as diurnal as a Gravesend barge. I hasten, as you do, to Florence or Siena, the rather to tell you a short story, from the interest you have given me in your safety.

At Siena I was tabled in the house of one Alberto Scipioni, an old Roman courtier in dangerous times; having been steward to the Duca di Pagliano, who with all his family were strangled, save this only man that escaped by foresight of the tempest. With him I had often much chat of those affairs, into which he took pleasure to look back from his native harbour; and, at my departure toward Rome (which had been the centre of his experience), I had won his confidence enough to beg his advice how I might carry myself there without offence of others or of mine own conscience. '*Signor Arrigo mio,*' says he, '*i pensieri stretti ed il viso sciolto* will go safely over the whole world.' Of which Delphian oracle (for so I have found it) your judgment doth need no commentary; and therefore, Sir, I will commit you, with it, to the best of all securities, God's dear love, remaining

Your friend, as much to command as any of longer date,

HENRY WOTTON."

Postscript.

"Sir: I have expressly sent this my footboy to prevent your departure without some acknowledgement from me of the receipt of your obliging letter; having myself through some business, I know not how, neglected the ordinary conveyance. In any part where I shall understand you fixed, I shall be glad and diligent to entertain you with home-novelties, even for some fomentation of our friendship, too soon interrupted in the cradle."

THE PERSONS.

THE ATTENDANT SPIRIT, afterwards in the
  habit of THYRSIS.

COMUS, with his Crew.

THE LADY.

FIRST BROTHER.

SECOND BROTHER.

SABRINA, the Nymph.

The Chief Persons which presented were :—

  The Lord Brackley ;
  Mr Thomas Egerton, his Brother ;
  The Lady Alice Egerton.

COMUS.

The first Scene discovers a wild wood.

The ATTENDANT SPIRIT *descends or enters.*

BEFORE the starry threshold of Jove's court
My mansion is, where those immortal shapes
Of bright aerial spirits live insphered
In regions mild of calm and serene air,
Above the smoke and stir of this dim spot
Which men call Earth, and with low-thoughted care,
Confined and pestered in this pinfold here,
Strive to keep up a frail and feverish being,
Unmindful of the crown that Virtue gives,
After this mortal change, to her true servants   10
Amongst the enthroned gods on sainted seats.
Yet some there be that by due steps aspire
To lay their just hands on that golden key
That opes the palace of eternity.
To such my errand is; and, but for such,
I would not soil these pure ambrosial weeds
With the rank vapours of this sin-worn mould.
   But to my task. Neptune, besides the sway
Of every salt flood and each ebbing stream,
Took in by lot, 'twixt high and nether Jove,   20
Imperial rule of all the sea-girt isles
That, like to rich and various gems, inlay

The unadorned bosom of the deep;
Which he, to grace his tributary gods,
By course commits to several government,
And gives them leave to wear their sapphire crowns
And wield their little tridents. But this Isle,
The greatest and the best of all the main,
He quarters to his blue-haired deities;
And all this tract that fronts the falling sun   30
A noble Peer of mickle trust and power
Has in his charge, with tempered awe to guide
An old and haughty nation, proud in arms:
Where his fair offspring, nursed in princely lore,
Are coming to attend their father's state,
And new-intrusted sceptre; but their way
Lies through the perplexed paths of this drear wood,
The nodding horror of whose shady brows
Threats the forlorn and wandering passenger;
And here their tender age might suffer peril,   40
But that by quick command from sovran Jove
I was despatched for their defence and guard!
And listen why; for I will tell you now
What never yet was heard in tale or song,
From old or modern bard, in hall or bower.

   Bacchus, that first from out the purple grape
Crushed the sweet poison of misused wine,
After the Tuscan mariners transformed,
Coasting the Tyrrhene shore, as the winds listed,
On Circe's island fell. (Who knows not Circe,   50
The daughter of the Sun, whose charmed cup
Whoever tasted lost his upright shape,
And downward fell into a grovelling swine?)
This nymph, that gazed upon his clustering locks,
With ivy berries wreathed, and his blithe youth,
Had by him, ere he parted thence, a son
Much like his father, but his mother more,

Whom therefore she brought up, and Comus named :
Who, ripe and frolic of his full-grown age,
Roving the Celtic and Iberian fields,   60
At last betakes him to this ominous wood,
And, in thick shelter of black shades imbowered,
Excels his mother at her mighty art ;
Offering to every weary traveller
His orient liquor in a crystal glass,
To quench the drouth of Phœbus ; which as they taste
(For most do taste through fond intemperate thirst),
Soon as the potion works, their human countenance,
The express resemblance of the gods, is changed
Into some brutish form of wolf, or bear,   70
Or ounce, or tiger, hog, or bearded goat,
All other parts remaining as they were.
And they, so perfect is their misery,
Not once perceive their foul disfigurement,
But boast themselves more comely than before,
And all their friends and native home forget,
To roll with pleasure in a sensual sty.
Therefore, when any favoured of high Jove
Chances to pass through this adventurous glade,
Swift as the sparkle of a glancing star   80
I shoot from heaven, to give him safe convoy,
As now I do. But first I must put off
These my sky-robes spun out of Iris' woof,
And take the weeds and likeness of a swain
That to the service of this house belongs,
Who with his soft pipe, and smooth-dittied song,
Well knows to still the wild winds when they roar,
And hush the waving woods ; nor of less faith,
And in this office of his mountain watch
Likeliest, and nearest to the present aid   90
Of this occasion. But I hear the tread
Of hateful steps ; I must be viewless now.

COMUS *enters, with a charming-rod in one hand, his
glass in the other; with him a rout of monsters,
headed like sundry sorts of wild beasts, but otherwise
like men and women, their apparel glistering: they
come in making a riotous and unruly noise, with
torches in their hands.*

Comus. The star that bids the shepherd fold
Now the top of heaven doth hold;
And the gilded car of day
His glowing axle doth allay
In the steep Atlantic stream;
And the slope sun his upward beam
Shoots against the dusky pole,
Pacing toward the other goal   100
Of his chamber in the east.
Meanwhile, welcome joy and feast,
Midnight shout and revelry,
Tipsy dance and jollity.
Braid your locks with rosy twine,
Dropping odours, dropping wine.
Rigour now is gone to bed;
And Advice with scrupulous head,
Strict Age, and sour Severity,
With their grave saws, in slumber lie.   110
We that are of purer fire
Imitate the starry quire,
Who, in their nightly watchful spheres,
Lead in swift round the months and years.
The sounds and seas, with all their finny drove,
Now to the moon in wavering morrice move;
And on the tawny sands and shelves
Trip the pert faeries and the dapper elves.
By dimpled brook and fountain-brim,
The wood-nymphs, decked with daisies trim,   120

Their merry wakes and pastimes keep:
What hath night to do with sleep?
Night hath better sweets to prove;
Venus now wakes, and wakens Love.
Come, let us our rites begin;
'Tis only daylight that makes sin,
Which these dun shades will ne'er report.
Hail, goddess of nocturnal sport,
Dark-veiled Cotytto, to whom the secret flame
Of midnight torches burns! mysterious dame,   130
That ne'er art called but when the dragon womb
Of Stygian darkness spets her thickest gloom,
And makes one blot of all the air!
Stay thy cloudy ebon chair,
Wherein thou ridest with Hecate, and befriend
Us thy vowed priests, till utmost end
Of all thy dues be done, and none left out;
Ere the blabbing eastern scout,
The nice Morn, on the Indian steep
From her cabined loop-hole peep,   140
And to the tell-tale Sun descry
Our concealed solemnity.
Come, knit hands, and beat the ground
In a light fantastic round.

The Measure.

Break off, break off! I feel the different pace
Of some chaste footing near about this ground.
Run to your shrouds within these brakes and trees;
Our number may affright. Some virgin sure
(For so I can distinguish by mine art)
Benighted in these woods! Now to my charms,   150
And to my wily trains: I shall ere long
Be well stocked with as fair a herd as grazed
About my mother Circe. Thus I hurl

My dazzling spells into the spongy air,
Of power to cheat the eye with blear illusion,
And give it false presentments, lest the place
And my quaint habits breed astonishment,
And put the damsel to suspicious flight;
Which must not be, for that's against my course:
I, under fair pretence of friendly ends, 160
And well-placed words of glozing courtesy,
Baited with reasons not unplausible,
Wind me into the easy-hearted man,
And hug him into snares. When once her eye
Hath met the virtue of this magic dust,
I shall appear some harmless villager,
Whom thrift keeps up about his country gear.
But here she comes; I fairly step aside,
And hearken, if I may her business hear.

The LADY *enters.*

Lady. This way the noise was, if mine ear be true,
My best guide now: methought it was the sound 171
Of riot and ill-managed merriment,
Such as the jocund flute or gamesome pipe
Stirs up among the loose unlettered hinds,
When, for their teeming flocks and granges full,
In wanton dance they praise the bounteous Pan,
And thank the gods amiss. I should be loth
To meet the rudeness and swilled insolence
Of such late wassailers; yet, oh! where else
Shall I inform my unacquainted feet 180
In the blind mazes of this tangled wood?
My brothers, when they saw me wearied out
With this long way, resolving here to lodge
Under the spreading favour of these pines,
Stepped, as they said, to the next thicket-side
To bring me berries, or such cooling fruit

As the kind hospitable woods provide.
They left me then when the gray-hooded Even,
Like a sad votarist in palmer's weed,
Rose from the hindmost wheels of Phœbus' wain. 190
But where they are, and why they came not back,
Is now the labour of my thoughts; 'tis likeliest
They had engaged their wandering steps too far,
And envious darkness, ere they could return,
Had stole them from me: else, O thievish Night,
Why shouldst thou, but for some felonious end,
In thy dark lantern thus close up the stars
That Nature hung in heaven, and filled their lamps
With everlasting oil, to give due light
To the misled and lonely traveller? 200
This is the place, as well as I may guess,
Whence even now the tumult of loud mirth
Was rife, and perfect in my listening ear;
Yet nought but single darkness do I find.
What might this be? A thousand fantasies
Begin to throng into my memory,
Of calling shapes, and beckoning shadows dire,
And airy tongues that syllable men's names
On sands and shores and desert wildernesses.
These thoughts may startle well, but not astound 210
The virtuous mind, that ever walks attended
By a strong siding champion, Conscience.
O, welcome, pure-eyed Faith, white-handed Hope,
Thou hovering angel girt with golden wings,
And thou unblemished form of Chastity!
I see ye visibly, and now believe
That He, the Supreme Good, to whom all things ill
Are but as slavish officers of vengeance,
Would send a glistering guardian, if need were,
To keep my life and honour unassailed— 220
Was I deceived, or did a sable cloud

Turn forth her silver lining on the night?
I did not err; there does a sable cloud
Turn forth her silver lining on the night,
And casts a gleam over this tufted grove.
I cannot hallo to my brothers, but
Such noise as I can make to be heard farthest
I'll venture; for my new-enlivened spirits
Prompt me, and they perhaps are not far off.

Song.

Sweet Echo, sweetest nymph, that liv'st unseen   230
    Within thy airy shell
  By slow Meander's margent green,
And in the violet-embroidered vale
    Where the love-lorn nightingale
Nightly to thee her sad song mourneth well:
Canst thou not tell me of a gentle pair
    That likest thy Narcissus are?
      O, if thou have
    Hid them in some flowery cave,
      Tell me but where,   240
Sweet Queen of parley, Daughter of the sphere!
  So may'st thou be translated to the skies,
And give resounding grace to all Heaven's harmonies!

  Comus. Can any mortal mixture of earth's mould
Breathe such divine enchanting ravishment?
Sure something holy lodges in that breast,
And with these raptures moves the vocal air
To testify his hidden residence.
How sweetly did they float upon the wings
Of silence, through the empty-vaulted night,   250
At every fall smoothing the raven down
Of darkness till it smiled! I have oft heard
My mother Circe with the Sirens three,
Amidst the flowery-kirtled Naiades,

Culling their potent herbs and baleful drugs;
Who, as they sung, would take the prisoned soul,
And lap it in Elysium: Scylla wept,
And chid her barking waves into attention,
And fell Charybdis murmured soft applause.
Yet they in pleasing slumber lulled the sense, 260
And in sweet madness robbed it of itself;
But such a sacred and home-felt delight,
Such sober certainty of waking bliss,
I never heard till now. I'll speak to her,
And she shall be my queen.—Hail, foreign wonder!
Whom certain these rough shades did never breed,
Unless the goddess that in rural shrine
Dwell'st here with Pan or Sylvan, by blest song
Forbidding every bleak unkindly fog
To touch the prosperous growth of this tall wood. 270
    Lady. Nay, gentle shepherd, ill is lost that praise
That is addressed to unattending ears :
Not any boast of skill, but extreme shift
How to regain my severed company,
Compelled me to awake the courteous Echo
To give me answer from her mossy couch.
    Comus. What chance, good Lady, hath bereft you thus?
    Lady. Dim darkness, and this leavy labyrinth.
    Comus. Could that divide you from near-ushering
        guides?
    Lady. They left me weary on a grassy turf. 280
    Comus. By falsehood, or discourtesy, or why?
    Lady. To seek i' the valley some cool friendly spring.
    Comus. And left your fair side all unguarded, Lady?
    Lady. They were but twain, and purposed quick return.
    Comus. Perhaps forestalling night prevented them.
    Lady. How easy my misfortune is to hit!
    Comus. Imports their loss, beside the present need?
    Lady. No less than if I should my brothers lose.

Comus. Were they of manly prime, or youthful bloom?
Lady. As smooth as Hebe's their unrazored lips. 290
Comus. Two such I saw, what time the laboured ox
In his loose traces from the furrow came,
And the swinked hedger at his supper sat.
I saw them under a green mantling vine,
That crawls along the side of yon small hill,
Plucking ripe clusters from the tender shoots ;
Their port was more than human, as they stood :
I took it for a faery vision
Of some gay creatures of the element,
That in the colours of the rainbow live,　　　300
And play i' the plighted clouds. I was awe-strook,
And, as I passed, I worshipped : if those you seek,
It were a journey like the path to Heaven,
To help you find them.
　　Lady.　　　　　　Gentle villager,
What readiest way would bring me to that place?
　Comus. Due west it rises from this shrubby point.
　Lady. To find out that, good shepherd, I suppose,
In such a scant allowance of star-light,
Would overtask the best land-pilot's art,
Without the sure guess of well-practised feet.　310
　Comus. I know each lane, and every alley green,
Dingle, or bushy dell, of this wild wood,
And every bosky bourn from side to side,
My daily walks and ancient neighbourhood ;
And if your stray attendance be yet lodged,
Or shroud within these limits, I shall know
Ere morrow wake, or the low-roosted lark
From her thatched pallet rouse : if otherwise,
I can conduct you, Lady, to a low
But loyal cottage, where you may be safe　　320
Till further quest.
　　Lady.　　　　Shepherd, I take thy word,

And trust thy honest-offered courtesy,
Which oft is sooner found in lowly sheds,
With smoky rafters, than in tapestry halls
And courts of princes, where it first was named,
And yet is most pretended. In a place
Less warranted than this, or less secure,
I cannot be, that I should fear to change it.
Eye me, blest Providence, and square my trial
To my proportioned strength! Shepherd, lead on.   330
                                        [*Exeunt.*

Enter the TWO BROTHERS.

  Elder Brother. Unmuffle, ye faint Stars; and thou,
           fair Moon,
Thou wont'st to love the traveller's benison,
Stoop thy pale visage through an amber cloud,
And disinherit Chaos, that reigns here
In double night of darkness and of shades;
Or, if your influence be quite dammed up
With black usurping mists, some gentle taper,
Though a rush-candle from the wicker hole
Of some clay habitation, visit us
With thy long levelled rule of streaming light,   340
And thou shalt be our star of Arcady,
Or Tyrian Cynosure.
  Second Brother.   Or, if our eyes
Be barred that happiness, might we but hear
The folded flocks, penned in their wattled cotes,
Or sound of pastoral reed with oaten stops,
Or whistle from the lodge, or village cock
Count the night-watches to his feathery dames,
'Twould be some solace yet, some little cheering,
In this close dungeon of innumerous boughs.
But, Oh, that hapless virgin, our lost sister!   350
Where may she wander now, whither betake her

From the chill dew, amongst rude burs and thistles?
Perhaps some cold bank is her bolster now,
Or 'gainst the rugged bark of some broad elm
Leans her unpillowed head, fraught with sad fears.
What if in wild amazement and affright,
Or, while we speak, within the direful grasp
Of savage hunger, or of savage heat!

    Eld. Bro. Peace, brother: be not over-exquisite
To cast the fashion of uncertain evils;   360
For, grant they be so, while they rest unknown,
What need a man forestall his date of grief,
And run to meet what he would most avoid?
Or, if they be but false alarms of fear,
How bitter is such self-delusion!
I do not think my sister so to seek,
Or so unprincipled in virtue's book,
And the sweet peace that goodness bosoms ever,
As that the single want of light and noise
(Not being in danger, as I trust she is not)   370
Could stir the constant mood of her calm thoughts,
And put them into misbecoming plight.
Virtue could see to do what Virtue would
By her own radiant light, though sun and moon
Were in the flat sea sunk. And Wisdom's self
Oft seeks to sweet retired solitude,
Where, with her best nurse, Contemplation,
She plumes her feathers, and lets grow her wings,
That in the various bustle of resort
Were all to-ruffled, and sometimes impaired.   380
He that has light within his own clear breast
May sit i' the centre, and enjoy bright day:
But he that hides a dark soul, and foul thoughts,
Benighted walks under the mid-day sun;
Himself is his own dungeon.

    Second Brother.   'Tis most true

That musing Meditation most affects
The pensive secrecy of desert cell,
Far from the cheerful haunt of men and herds,
And sits as safe as in a senate-house ;
For who would rob a hermit of his weeds,   390
His few books, or his beads, or maple dish,
Or do his gray hairs any violence ?
But Beauty, like the fair Hesperian tree
Laden with blooming gold, had need the guard
Of dragon-watch with unenchanted eye,
To save her blossoms, and defend her fruit,
From the rash hand of bold Incontinence.
You may as well spread out the unsunned heaps
Of miser's treasure by an outlaw's den,
And tell me it is safe, as bid me hope   400
Danger will wink on Opportunity,
And let a single helpless maiden pass
Uninjured in this wild surrounding waste.
Of night or loneliness it recks me not ;
I fear the dread events that dog them both,
Lest some ill-greeting touch attempt the person
Of our unowned sister.
   Elder Brother.   I do not, brother,
Infer as if I thought my sister's state
Secure without all doubt or controversy ;
Yet, where an equal poise of hope and fear   410
Does arbitrate the event, my nature is
That I incline to hope rather than fear,
And gladly banish squint suspicion.
My sister is not so defenceless left
As you imagine ; she has a hidden strength,
Which you remember not.
   Second Brother.   What hidden strength,
Unless the strength of Heaven, if you mean that ?
   Eld. Bro. I mean that too, but yet a hidden strength,

Which, if Heaven gave it, may be termed her own.
'Tis chastity, my brother, chastity: 420
She that has that is clad in complete steel,
And, like a quivered nymph with arrows keen,
May trace huge forests, and unharboured heaths,
Infamous hills, and sandy perilous wilds;
Where, through the sacred rays of chastity,
No savage fierce, bandite, or mountaineer,
Will dare to soil her virgin purity:
Yea, there where very desolation dwells,
By grots and caverns shagged with horrid shades,
She may pass on with unblenched majesty,   430
Be it not done in pride, or in presumption.
Some say no evil thing that walks by night,
In fog or fire, by lake or moorish fen,
Blue meagre hag, or stubborn unlaid ghost,
That breaks his magic chains at curfew time,
No goblin, or swart faery of the mine,
Hath hurtful power o'er true virginity.
Do ye believe me yet, or shall I call
Antiquity from the old schools of Greece
To testify the arms of chastity?   440
Hence had the huntress Dian her dread bow,
Fair silver-shafted queen for ever chaste,
Wherewith she tamed the brinded lioness
And spotted mountain-pard, but set at nought
The frivolous bolt of Cupid; gods and men
Feared her stern frown, and she was queen o' the
    woods.
What was that snaky-headed Gorgon shield
That wise Minerva wore, unconquered virgin,
Wherewith she freezed her foes to congealed stone,
But rigid looks of chaste austerity,   450
And noble grace that dashed brute violence
With sudden adoration and blank awe?

So dear to Heaven is saintly chastity,
That, when a soul is found sincerely so,
A thousand liveried angels lackey her,
Driving far off each thing of sin and guilt,
And in clear dream and solemn vision
Tell her of things that no gross ear can hear;
Till oft converse with heavenly habitants
Begin to cast a beam on the outward shape,   460
The unpolluted temple of the mind,
And turns it by degrees to the soul's essence,
Till all be made immortal. But when lust,
By unchaste looks, loose gestures, and foul talk,
But most by lewd and lavish act of sin,
Lets in defilement to the inward parts,
The soul grows clotted by contagion,
Imbodies, and imbrutes, till she quite lose
The divine property of her first being.
Such are those thick and gloomy shadows damp   470
Oft seen in charnel-vaults and sepulchres,
Lingering and sitting by a new-made grave,
As loth to leave the body that it loved,
And linked itself by carnal sensualty
To a degenerate and degraded state.
   Second Brother.   How charming is divine Philosophy!
Not harsh and crabbed, as dull fools suppose,
But musical as is Apollo's lute,
And a perpetual feast of nectared sweets,
Where no crude surfeit reigns.
   Elder Brother.   List! list! I hear 480
Some far-off hallo break the silent air.
   Sec. Bro.   Methought so too; what should it be?
   Elder Brother.   For certain,
Either some one, like us, night-foundered here,
Or else some neighbour woodman, or, at worst,
Some roving robber calling to his fellows.

Second Brother. Heaven keep my sister! Again, again,
     and near!
Best draw, and stand upon our guard.
     Elder Brother.   I'll hallo.
If he be friendly, he comes well: if not,
Defence is a good cause, and Heaven be for us!

Enter the ATTENDANT SPIRIT, *habited like a shepherd.*

That hallo I should know. What are you? speak.   490
Come not too near; you fall on iron stakes else.
     Spirit. What voice is that? my young Lord? speak
     again.
     Sec. Bro. O brother, 'tis my father's Shepherd, sure.
     Eld. Bro. Thyrsis! whose artful strains have oft delayed
The huddling brook to hear his madrigal,
And sweetened every musk-rose of the dale.
How camest thou here, good swain? hath any ram
Slipped from the fold, or young kid lost his dam,
Or straggling wether the pent flock forsook?
How couldst thou find this dark sequestered nook?   500
     Spirit. O my loved master's heir, and his next joy,
I came not here on such a trivial toy
As a strayed ewe, or to pursue the stealth
Of pilfering wolf; not all the fleecy wealth
That doth enrich these downs is worth a thought
To this my errand, and the care it brought.
But, Oh! my virgin Lady, where is she?
How chance she is not in your company?
     Elder Brother. To tell thee sadly, Shepherd, without
     blame
Or our neglect, we lost her as we came.   510
     Spirit. Ay me unhappy! then my fears are true.
     Elder Brother. What fears, good Thyrsis? Prithee
     briefly shew.
     Spirit. I'll tell ye; 'tis not vain or fabulous,

(Though so esteemed by shallow ignorance)
What the sage poets, taught by the heavenly Muse,
Storied of old in high immortal verse
Of dire Chimeras and enchanted isles,
And rifted rocks whose entrance leads to Hell;
For such there be, but unbelief is blind.
    Within the navel of this hideous wood,   520
Immured in cypress shades, a sorcerer dwells,
Of Bacchus and of Circe born, great Comus,
Deep skilled in all his mother's witcheries;
And here to every thirsty wanderer
By sly enticement gives his baneful cup,
With many murmurs mixed, whose pleasing poison
The visage quite transforms of him that drinks,
And the inglorious likeness of a beast
Fixes instead, unmoulding reason's mintage
Charactered in the face. This have I learnt   530
Tending my flocks hard by i' the hilly crofts
That brow this bottom glade; whence night by night
He and his monstrous rout are heard to howl
Like stabled wolves, or tigers at their prey,
Doing abhorred rites to Hecate
In their obscured haunts of inmost bowers.
Yet have they many baits and guileful spells
To inveigle and invite the unwary sense
Of them that pass unweeting by the way.
This evening late, by then the chewing flocks   540
Had ta'en their supper on the savoury herb
Of knot-grass dew-besprent, and were in fold,
I sat me down to watch upon a bank
With ivy canopied, and interwove
With flaunting honeysuckle, and began,
Wrapt in a pleasing fit of melancholy,
To meditate my rural minstrelsy,
Till fancy had her fill; but ere a close

The wonted roar was up amidst the woods,
And filled the air with barbarous dissonance ;   550
At which I ceased, and listened them a while,
Till an unusual stop of sudden silence
Gave respite to the drowsy-flighted steeds
That draw the litter of close-curtained Sleep.
At last a soft and solemn-breathing sound
Rose like a steam of rich distilled perfumes,
And stole upon the air, that even Silence
Was took ere she was ware, and wished she might
Deny her nature, and be never more,
Still to be so displaced. I was all ear,   560
And took in strains that might create a soul
Under the ribs of Death : but, Oh ! ere long
Too well I did perceive it was the voice
Of my most honoured Lady, your dear sister.
Amazed I stood, harrowed with grief and fear ;
And 'O poor hapless nightingale,' thought I,
'How sweet thou sing'st, how near the deadly snare !'
Then down the lawns I ran with headlong haste,
Through paths and turnings often trod by day,
Till, guided by mine ear, I found the place   570
Where that damned wizard, hid in sly disguise
(For so by certain signs I knew), had met
Already, ere my best speed could prevent,
The aidless innocent lady, his wished prey ;
Who gently asked if he had seen such two,
Supposing him some neighbour villager.
Longer I durst not stay, but soon I guessed
Ye were the two she meant ; with that I sprung
Into swift flight, till I had found you here ;
But further know I not.
   Second Brother.   O Night and Shades,   580
How are ye joined with hell in triple knot
Against the unarmed weakness of one virgin,

Alone and helpless! Is this the confidence
You gave me, brother?
 Elder Brother. Yes, and keep it still;
Lean on it safely; not a period
Shall be unsaid for me. Against the threats
Of malice or of sorcery, or that power
Which erring men call Chance, this I hold firm:
Virtue may be assailed, but never hurt,
Surprised by unjust force, but not enthralled; 590
Yea, even that which Mischief meant most harm
Shall in the happy trial prove most glory.
But evil on itself shall back recoil,
And mix no more with goodness, when at last,
Gathered like scum, and settled to itself,
It shall be in eternal restless change
Self-fed and self-consumed: if this fail,
The pillared firmament is rottenness,
And earth's base built on stubble. But come, let's on!
Against the opposing will and arm of Heaven 600
May never this just sword be lifted up;
But, for that damned magician, let him be girt
With all the griesly legions that troop
Under the sooty flag of Acheron,
Harpies and Hydras, or all the monstrous forms
'Twixt Africa and Ind, I'll find him out,
And force him to return his purchase back,
Or drag him by the curls to a foul death,
Cursed as his life.
 Spirit. Alas! good venturous youth,
I love thy courage yet, and bold emprise; 610
But here thy sword can do thee little stead:
Far other arms and other weapons must
Be those that quell the might of hellish charms;
He with his bare wand can unthread thy joints,
And crumble all thy sinews.

Elder Brother.   Why, prithee, Shepherd,
How durst thou then thyself approach so near
As to make this relation?
    Spirit.   Care and utmost shifts
How to secure the Lady from surprisal
Brought to my mind a certain shepherd lad,
Of small regard to see to, yet well skilled   620
In every virtuous plant and healing herb
That spreads her verdant leaf to the morning ray :
He loved me well, and oft would beg me sing ;
Which when I did, he on the tender grass
Would sit, and hearken even to ecstasy,
And in requital ope his leathern scrip,
And show me simples of a thousand names,
Telling their strange and vigorous faculties.
Amongst the rest a small unsightly root,
But of divine effect, he culled me out ;   630
The leaf was darkish, and had prickles on it,
But in another country, as he said,
Bore a bright golden flower, but not in this soil :
Unknown, and like esteemed, and the dull swain
Treads on it daily with his clouted shoon ;
And yet more med'cinal is it than that Moly
That Hermes once to wise Ulysses gave.
He called it Hæmony, and gave it me,
And bade me keep it as of sovran use
'Gainst all enchantments, mildew blast, or damp,   640
Or ghastly Furies' apparition.
I pursed it up, but little reckoning made,
Till now that this extremity compelled :
But now I find it true ; for by this means
I knew the foul enchanter, though disguised,
Entered the very lime-twigs of his spells,
And yet came off. If you have this about you
(As I will give you when we go) you may

Boldly assault the necromancer's hall;
Where if he be, with dauntless hardihood 650
And brandished blade rush on him : break his glass,
And shed the luscious liquor on the ground,
But seize his wand; though he and his curst crew
Fierce sign of battle make, and menace high,
Or, like the sons of Vulcan, vomit smoke,
Yet will they soon retire, if he but shrink.
   Eld. Bro. Thyrsis, lead on apace; I'll follow thee;
And some good angel bear a shield before us !

*The Scene changes to a stately palace, set out with all
   manner of deliciousness: soft music, tables spread
   with all dainties.* COMUS *appears with his rabble,
   and* THE LADY *set in an enchanted chair; to whom
   he offers his glass, which she puts by, and goes about
   to rise.*

   Comus. Nay, Lady, sit : if I but wave this wand,
Your nerves are all chained up in alabaster, 660
And you a statue, or as Daphne was,
Root-bound, that fled Apollo.
   Lady.   Fool, do not boast :
Thou canst not touch the freedom of my mind
With all thy charms, although this corporal rind
Thou hast immanacled, while Heaven sees good.
   Comus. Why are you vexed, Lady? why do you
   frown?
Here dwell no frowns, nor anger ; from these gates
Sorrow flies far. See, here be all the pleasures
That fancy can beget on youthful thoughts,
When the fresh blood grows lively, and returns 670
Brisk as the April buds in primrose season.
And first behold this cordial julep here,
That flames and dances in his crystal bounds,

With spirits of balm and fragrant syrups mixed.
Not that Nepenthes which the wife of Thone
In Egypt gave to Jove-born Helena
Is of such power to stir up joy as this,
To life so friendly, or so cool to thirst.
Why should you be so cruel to yourself,
And to those dainty limbs, which Nature lent   680
For gentle usage and soft delicacy?
But you invert the covenants of her trust,
And harshly deal, like an ill borrower,
With that which you received on other terms,
Scorning the unexempt condition
By which all mortal frailty must subsist,
Refreshment after toil, ease after pain,
That have been tired all day without repast,
And timely rest have wanted; but, fair virgin,
This will restore all soon.

    Lady.   'Twill not, false traitor! 690
'Twill not restore the truth and honesty
That thou hast banished from thy tongue with lies.
Was this the cottage and the safe abode
Thou told'st me of? What grim aspects are these,
These ugly-headed monsters? Mercy guard me!
Hence with thy brewed enchantments, foul deceiver!
Hast thou betrayed my credulous innocence
With vizored falsehood and base forgery?
And wouldst thou seek again to trap me here
With lickerish baits, fit to ensnare a brute?   700
Were it a draught for Juno when she banquets,
I would not taste thy treasonous offer: none
But such as are good men can give good things;
And that which is not good is not delicious
To a well-governed and wise appetite.

    Comus. O foolishness of men! that lend their ears
To those budge doctors of the Stoic fur,

And fetch their precepts from the Cynic tub,
Praising the lean and sallow Abstinence !
Wherefore did Nature pour her bounties forth   710
With such a full and unwithdrawing hand,
Covering the earth with odours, fruits, and flocks
Thronging the seas with spawn innumerable,
But all to please and sate the curious taste?
And set to work millions of spinning worms,
That in their green shops weave the smooth-haired silk,
To deck her sons ; and, that no corner might
Be vacant of her plenty, in her own loins
She hutched the all-worshipped ore and precious gems,
To store her children with. If all the world   720
Should in a pet of temperance feed on pulse,
Drink the clear stream, and nothing wear but frieze,
The All-giver would be unthanked, would be unpraised,
Not half his riches known, and yet despised ;
And we should serve him as a grudging master,
As a penurious niggard of his wealth,
And live like Nature's bastards, not her sons,
Who would be quite surcharged with her own weight,
And strangled with her waste fertility :
The earth cumbered, and the winged air darked with
      plumes,   730
The herds would over-multitude their lords ;
The sea o'erfraught would swell, and the unsought
      diamonds
Would so emblaze the forehead of the deep,
And so bestud with stars, that they below
Would grow inured to light, and come at last
To gaze upon the sun with shameless brows.
List, Lady ; be not coy, and be not cozened
With that same vaunted name, Virginity.
Beauty is Nature's coin ; must not be hoarded,
But must be current ; and the good thereof   740

Consists in mutual and partaken bliss,
Unsavoury in the enjoyment of itself:
If you let slip time, like a neglected rose
It withers on the stalk with languished head.
Beauty is Nature's brag, and must be shown
In courts, at feasts, and high solemnities,
Where most may wonder at the workmanship:
It is for homely features to keep home,
They had their name thence; coarse complexions
And cheeks of sorry grain will serve to ply   750
The sampler, and to tease the huswife's wool.
What need a vermeil-tinctured lip for that,
Love-darting eyes, or tresses like the morn?
There was another meaning in these gifts;
Think what, and be advised; you are but young yet.
    Lady. I had not thought to have unlocked my lips
In this unhallowed air, but that this juggler
Would think to charm my judgment, as mine eyes,
Obtruding false rules pranked in reason's garb.
I hate when Vice can bolt her arguments   760
And Virtue has no tongue to check her pride.
Impostor! do not charge most innocent Nature,
As if she would her children should be riotous
With her abundance; she, good cateress,
Means her provision only to the good,
That live according to her sober laws,
And holy dictate of spare Temperance.
If every just man that now pines with want
Had but a moderate and beseeming share
Of that which lewdly-pampered Luxury   770
Now heaps upon some few with vast excess,
Nature's full blessings would be well-dispensed
In unsuperfluous even proportion,
And she no whit encumbered with her store;
And then the Giver would be better thanked,

His praise due paid: for swinish gluttony
Ne'er looks to Heaven amidst his gorgeous feast,
But with besotted base ingratitude
Crams, and blasphemes his Feeder. Shall I go on?
Or have I said enow? To him that dares   780
Arm his profane tongue with contemptuous words
Against the sun-clad power of chastity,
Fain would I something say;—yet to what end?
Thou hast nor ear, nor soul, to apprehend
The sublime notion and high mystery
That must be uttered to unfold the sage
And serious doctrine of Virginity;
And thou art worthy that thou shouldst not know
More happiness than this thy present lot.
Enjoy your dear wit, and gay rhetoric,   790
That hath so well been taught her dazzling fence;
Thou art not fit to hear thyself convinced:
Yet, should I try, the uncontrolled worth
Of this pure cause would kindle my rapt spirits
To such a flame of sacred vehemence,
That dumb things would be moved to sympathize,
And the brute Earth would lend her nerves, and shake,
Till all thy magic structures, reared so high,
Were shattered into heaps o'er thy false head.
    Comus. She fables not. I feel that I do fear   800
Her words set off by some superior power;
And, though not mortal, yet a cold shuddering dew
Dips me all o'er, as when the wrath of Jove
Speaks thunder and the chains of Erebus
To some of Saturn's crew. I must dissemble,
And try her yet more strongly.—Come, no more!
This is mere moral babble, and direct
Against the canon laws of our foundation;
I must not suffer this; yet 'tis but the lees
And settlings of a melancholy blood: 810

But this will cure all straight; one sip of this
Will bathe the drooping spirits in delight
Beyond the bliss of dreams. Be wise, and taste ...

The BROTHERS *rush in with swords drawn, wrest his
glass out of his hand, and break it against the
ground: his rout make sign of resistance, but are all
driven in. The* ATTENDANT SPIRIT *comes in.*

Spirit. What! have you let the false enchanter scape?
O ye mistook; ye should have snatched his wand,
And bound him fast: without his rod reversed,
And backward mutters of dissevering power,
We cannot free the Lady that sits here
In stony fetters fixed and motionless.
Yet stay: be not disturbed; now I bethink me,   820
Some other means I have which may be used,
Which once of Melibœus old I learnt,
The soothest shepherd that e'er piped on plains.
    There is a gentle nymph not far from hence,
That with moist curb sways the smooth Severn stream:
Sabrina is her name: a virgin pure;
Whilom she was the daughter of Locrine,
That had the sceptre from his father Brute.
She, guiltless damsel, flying the mad pursuit
Of her enraged stepdame, Guendolen,   830
Commended her fair innocence to the flood
That stayed her flight with his cross-flowing course.
The water-nymphs, that in the bottom played,
Held up their pearled wrist, and took her in,
Bearing her straight to aged Nereus' hall;
Who, piteous of her woes, reared her lank head,
And gave her to his daughters to imbathe
In nectared lavers strewed with asphodil,
And through the porch and inlet of each scnse

Dropt in ambrosial oils, till she revived,   840
And underwent a quick immortal change,
Made goddess of the river. Still she retains
Her maiden gentleness, and oft at eve
Visits the herds along the twilight meadows,
Helping all urchin blasts, and ill-luck signs
That the shrewd meddling elf delights to make,
Which she with precious vialed liquors heals:
For which the shepherds at their festivals
Carol her goodness loud in rustic lays,
And throw sweet garland wreaths into her stream   850
Of pansies, pinks, and gaudy daffodils.
And, as the old swain said, she can unlock
The clasping charm, and thaw the numbing spell,
If she be right invoked in warbled song;
For maidenhood she loves, and will be swift
To aid a virgin, such as was herself,
In hard-besetting need: this will I try,
And add the power of some adjuring verse.

Song.

Sabrina fair,
    Listen where thou art sitting   860
Under the glassy, cool, translucent wave,
    In twisted braids of lilies knitting
The loose train of thy amber-dropping hair;
    Listen for dear honour's sake,
    Goddess of the silver lake,
        Listen and save!
Listen and appear to us,
In name of great Oceanus,
By the earth-shaking Neptune's mace,
And Tethys' grave majestic pace;   870
By hoary Nereus' wrinkled look,
And the Carpathian wizard's hook;

By scaly Triton's winding shell,
And old soothsaying Glaucus' spell;
By Leucothea's lovely hands,
And her son that rules the strands;
By Thetis' tinsel-slippered feet,
And the songs of Sirens sweet;
By dead Parthenope's dear tomb,
And fair Ligea's golden comb,   880
Wherewith she sits on diamond rocks
Sleeking her soft alluring locks;
By all the nymphs that nightly dance
Upon thy streams with wily glance;
Rise, rise, and heave thy rosy head
From thy coral-paven bed,
And bridle in thy headlong wave,
Till thou our summons answered have.
                              Listen and save!

SABRINA *rises, attended by Water-nymphs, and sings.*

By the rushy-fringed bank,   890
Where grows the willow and the osier dank,
    My sliding chariot stays,
Thick set with agate, and the azurn sheen
Of turkis blue, and emerald green,
    That in the channel strays:
Whilst from off the waters fleet
Thus I set my printless feet
O'er the cowslip's velvet head,
    That bends not as I tread.
Gentle swain, at thy request   900
        I am here!
    Spirit. Goddess dear,
We implore thy powerful hand
To undo the charmed band

Of true virgin here distressed,
Through the force and through the wile
Of unblessed enchanter vile.
    Sabrina. Shepherd, 'tis my office best
To help ensnared chastity :
Brightest Lady, look on me.   910
Thus I sprinkle on thy breast
Drops that from my fountain pure
I have kept of precious cure ;
Thrice upon thy finger's tip,
Thrice upon thy rubied lip :
Next this marbled venomed seat,
Smeared with gums of glutinous heat,
I touch with chaste palms moist and cold.
Now the spell hath lost his hold ;
And I must haste ere morning hour   920
To wait in Amphitrite's bower.

SABRINA *descends, and* THE LADY *rises out of her seat.*

    Spirit. Virgin, daughter of Locrine,
Sprung of old Anchises' line,
May thy brimmed waves for this
Their full tribute never miss
From a thousand petty rills,
That tumble down the snowy hills :
Summer drouth or singed air
Never scorch thy tresses fair,
Nor wet October's torrent flood   930
Thy molten crystal fill with mud ;
May thy billows roll ashore
The beryl and the golden ore ;
May thy lofty head be crowned
With many a tower and terrace round,
And here and there thy banks upon

With groves of myrrh and cinnamon.
   Come, Lady, while Heaven lends us grace,
Let us fly this cursed place,
Lest the sorcerer us entice   940
With some other new device.
Not a waste or needless sound
Till we come to holier ground ;
I shall be your faithful guide
Through this gloomy covert wide ;
And not many furlongs thence
Is your Father's residence,
Where this night are met in state
Many a friend to gratulate
His wished presence, and beside   950
All the swains that there abide
With jigs and rural dance resort ;
We shall catch them at their sport,
And our sudden coming there
Will double all their mirth and cheer.
Come, let us haste ; the stars grow high,
But Night sits monarch yet in the mid sky.

*The Scene changes, presenting Ludlow Town and the
President's Castle : then come in Country Dancers ;
after them the* ATTENDANT SPIRIT, *with the two*
BROTHERS *and* THE LADY.

Song.

   Spirit. Back, shepherds, back ! enough your
     play,
Till next sun-shine holiday :
Here be, without duck or nod,   960
Other trippings to be trod
Of lighter toes, and such court guise
As Mercury did first devise

With the mincing Dryades
On the lawns and on the leas.

*This second Song presents them to their Father and
Mother.*

Noble Lord, and Lady bright,
I have brought ye new delight;
Here behold so goodly grown
Three fair branches of your own:
Heaven hath timely tried their youth, 970
Their faith, their patience, and their truth,
And sent them here through hard assays
With a crown of deathless praise,
To triumph in victorious dance
O'er sensual folly and intemperance.

The dances ended, the SPIRIT *epiloguizes.*

Spirit. To the ocean now I fly,
And those happy climes that lie
Where day never shuts his eye,
Up in the broad fields of the sky;
There I suck the liquid air, 980
All amidst the gardens fair
Of Hesperus, and his daughters three
That sing about the golden tree.
Along the crisped shades and bowers
Revels the spruce and jocund Spring;
The Graces and the rosy-bosomed Hours
Thither all their bounties bring;
There eternal Summer dwells,
And west winds with musky wing
About the cedarn alleys fling 990
Nard and cassia's balmy smells.

Iris there with humid bow
Waters the odorous banks, that blow
Flowers of more mingled hue
Than her purfled scarf can shew;
And drenches with Elysian dew
(List, mortals, if your ears be true)
Beds of hyacinth and roses,
Where young Adonis oft reposes,
Waxing well of his deep wound   1000
In slumber soft, and on the ground
Sadly sits the Assyrian queen :
But far above in spangled sheen
Celestial Cupid, her famed son advanced,
Holds his dear Psyche sweet entranced,
After her wandering labours long,
Till free consent the gods among
Make her his eternal bride,
And from her fair unspotted side
Two blissful twins are to be born,   1010
Youth and Joy; so Jove hath sworn.
  But now my task is smoothly done :
I can fly, or I can run,
Quickly to the green earth's end,
Where the bowed welkin slow doth bend,
And from thence can soar as soon
To the corners of the moon.
  Mortals, that would follow me,
Love Virtue : she alone is free ;
She can teach ye how to climb   1020
Higher than the sphery chime ;
Or if Virtue feeble were,
Heaven itself would stoop to her.

NOTES.

LAWES'S DEDICATION OF THE FIRST EDITION OF COMUS.

Henry Lawes, 1595—1662, sometime a "Gentleman of the Chapel Royal" (i.e. one of the royal choir), and a member of the king's "private music" (orchestra), was the chief composer of his age. He was specially noted as a composer of incidental music for Masques and of songs. He composed in 1633 part of the music for Shirley's great Masque *The Triumph of Peace*, and all the music for Carew's equally famous *Cælum Britannicum*. He wrote the music for *Comus* (and probably for *Arcades*), acted the part of "the Attendant Spirit" when the piece was first performed at Ludlow Castle in 1634, and was responsible for the publication of the first edition in 1637. He seems to have been one of Milton's earliest and most intimate friends, thanks, no doubt, to their common love of music.

Milton addressed the following Sonnet to him.

"TO MR H. LAWES ON HIS AIRS.

HARRY, whose tuneful and well-measured song
　　First taught our English music how to span
　　Words with just note and accent, not to scan
　　With Midas' ears, committing short and long,
Thy worth and skill exempts thee from the throng,
　　With praise enough for Envy to look wan ;
　　To after age thou shalt be writ the man
　　That with smooth air couldst humour best our tongue.

Thou honour'st verse, and verse must lend her wing
    To honour thee, the priest of Phœbus' quire,
    That tunest their happiest lines in hymn or story.
Dante shall give Fame leave to set thee higher
    Than his Casella, whom he wooed to sing,
    Met in the milder shades of Purgatory."

This Sonnet appeared as an introduction to a volume of "Choice Psalmes, put into Musick for three Voices: composed by Henry and William Lawes, Brothers, and Servants to his Majestie: 1648." The date of the composition of the Sonnet was Feb. 1646, as we learn from the Cambridge MS. Its familiar tone shows that the intimacy between the poet and the musician had not been affected by political differences, though Lawes, like his brother (who fell fighting for the king at Chester in 1645), was an ardent Royalist, and the volume of *Psalms* to which Milton's poem was prefixed was dedicated to Charles. After 1648 we do not hear of Lawes in connection with Milton, so that the force of circumstances may have driven them apart. It is significant that Lawes's dedication of *Comus*, which was reprinted in the 1645 edition of the poem, was omitted from the 1673 edition; though the omission may have been due to another cause.

The first four lines of the Sonnet, which should be compared with *Comus*, 86—88 and 494—496, give a very precise and musicianly description of Lawes's songs. He was content to make his music subordinate to the words, preserving their rhythm and accent with fidelity; so that the poetry, not the music (very often, a kind of recitative), was the chief element. This quality explains his great popularity with the poets of the period, many of whom, e.g. Herrick, Cartwright, Waller, had songs set to music by him. See Grove's *Dictionary of Music*.

Lord Brackley. The second Earl of Bridgewater, born in 1622; he succeeded his father in 1649, and died in 1686. This dedication was omitted (as we have said) from the edition of 1673; not unnaturally, since the Earl and the poet had taken opposite sides in the civil troubles. The former was arrested in 1651 on suspicion of being a Royalist. Milton's polemical tract *Pro Populo Anglicano Defensio* appeared in that year, and Todd says that the Earl of Bridgewater wrote on the title-page of his copy "Liber igne, author furca dignissimi" (i.e. 'the book well deserves burning and the author hanging'). For the rest he seems to have been a genial, learned man, who patronised literature and "delighted much in his library." See the *National Dictionary of Biography*. Of the younger brother, Mr Thomas Egerton, who took part in the Masque, little is known. The sister, Lady Alice, married Richard Vaughan, Earl of Carberry.

SIR HENRY WOTTON'S LETTER.

This letter is interesting as one of the earliest extant testimonies to Milton's genius. That he valued it much and thought that it would be a weighty recommendation of *Comus* is shown by his causing it to be prefixed to the 1645 edition of the poem. And in the *Second Defence* he says: "On my departure for Italy, the celebrated Henry Wotton gave me a signal proof of his regard, in an elegant letter which he wrote, not only breathing the warmest friendship, but containing some maxims of conduct which I found very useful in my travels" (*P. W.* I. 255).

Sir Henry Wotton, 1568—1639, was a man of some note in diplomacy and literature. He represented the English Court at Venice for some years; and afterwards (1625) became Provost of Eton, and took orders in the Church. He was a friend of Isaac Walton, who wrote his life. Wotton's chief work was published posthumously in 1651, under a title which explains its miscellaneous contents: "*Reliquiæ Wottonianæ;* or, a Collection of Lives, Letters, Poems, with Characters of sundry Personages, and other incomparable Pieces of Language and Art: By the curious Pencil of the ever-memorable Sir Henry Wotton, Knt., late Provost of Eaton College, 1651."

At least one of his poems ("You meaner beauties of the night") is familiar to lovers of Jacobean verse; and his definition of an ambassador as "an honest man sent to lie abroad for the good of his country" is still fresh. The *équivoque* had more point then than now, because "to lie" was technically used of an ambassador's residence abroad (Hannah). Wotton seems to have had a turn for aphorism. His favourite motto—engraved on his tombstone—was *disputandi pruritus ecclesiarum scabies* ('an itching for discussion is the mania of churches'). Sir

Henry Wotton admirably represents the type of courtier, wit and scholar. A sympathetic account of his career was published by Dr A. W. Ward; and recently his letters have been edited elaborately, with a full *Life*, for the Clarendon Press.

2. Horton being so close to Eton, it is curious that Sir Henry had not met his neighbour between 1632 and 1638.

6. *Mr H.* Commonly identified, and no doubt rightly, with the Broad Church divine John Hales, who was for some years a Fellow of Eton and Canon of Windsor. His learning won for him the title "the ever-memorable." There are allusions to him in Wotton's *Reliquiæ*.

10. *banded*, discussed.

16. *Doric*, i.e. Theocritean. Cf. *Lyc.* 189, "With eager thought warbling his Doric lay." Wotton shows his critical faculty in singling out the lyric portions of *Comus* for special commendation. Contrast Johnson's criticism.

23. *Mr R.* This "common friend" was probably John Rouse, of Oriel College, sometime (1620—1652) Bodley's Librarian. Milton had been incorporated M.A. at Oxford in 1635, according to the common practice, and on one of his visits to the University must have found his way to the Bodleian Library. Some years later (1647) the poet addressed Rouse in an elaborate Latin ode, celebrating the blissful silence and treasures of the great Library.

in the very close. Sir Henry Wotton means that a copy of Lawes's edition of *Comus* was inserted at the end of a volume of poems by "the late R": probably the Cambridge poet Thomas Randolph, who died in 1634 and whose poems were published by his brother in 1638, the year in which Sir Henry wrote the letter. Randolph was one of the ablest of the followers (intellectual "sons," as they called themselves) of Ben Jonson, and wrote several amusing plays. He was contemporary with Milton at Cambridge.

26. *con la bocca dolce*, i.e. with a pleasant taste in the mouth. Cf. French *bonne bouche*.

27, 28. Sir Henry modestly implies that he has more right to speak as an authority on travel than on literature.

29. *blanch*, omit, pass by. If we used the verb at all we should treat it as intransitive, inserting *from*.

Paris. Milton arrived there in April or May, 1638. He

seems to have stayed some time, not reaching Florence till August.

30. *Mr M. B.* Identified with Michael Branthwaite. Sir Henry Wotton mentions him in the *Reliquiæ* as "heretofore his Majesties Agent in Venice, a gentleman of approved confidence and sincerity," p. 546. This was in 1626. Afterwards Branthwaite became diplomatic agent at Paris.

Page 5, line 1. Lord S., i.e. Lord Scudamore, son of the English ambassador, Viscount Scudamore, who showed Milton much courtesy in Paris; as we learn from his *Second Defence of the People of England.* (This was one of Milton's political treatises, written in Latin to justify the English Civil War, and more especially the execution of Charles I., in the eyes of Europe. Milton's first pamphlet on the subject had elicited violent attacks upon himself, his life and character; in his reply he gave a sketch of his career. The *Second Defence* therefore has very great autobiographical interest.)

governor; we should say 'tutor.'

7. *Marseilles...to Genoa.* The route that Addison took; see his *Travels.* But Milton entered Italy by way of Nice, coasted thence to Genoa, and went on to Florence, the favourite resting-place of English travellers, where he spent some months.

8, 9. *a Gravesend barge.* Cf. Hasted's *History of Kent,* vol. I. p. 450: "King Richard II. granted to the *Abbat* and *Convent* of *St Mary Graces,* that the inhabitants of *Gravesend* and *Milton* should have the sole privilege of carrying passengers by water from hence to *London,* on condition that they should provide boats for that purpose, and carry all passengers either at 2*d.* per head with their bundle, or let the hire of the whole boat at 4*s.* This charter was confirmed several times afterwards by succeeding kings, and under proper regulation by the legislature they still (1778) enjoy the privilege."

12. *At Siena.* This was in the autumn of 1592. "I am here," Sir Henry writes to Lord Zouch from Siena, Oct. 25, 1592, "by the means of certain Persons (to whom I was recommended) gotten into the House of Scipione Alberti, an ancient Courtier of the Popes, and a Gentleman of this Town, at whose Table I live." In a letter dated August 22, 1593, he mentions his Siena host again, and also refers to the Duke of Pagliano.

17, 18. *at my departure.* Evidently the story that follows was a favourite with Sir Henry; he tells it in the *Reliquiæ.*

21, 22. *i pensieri* etc. "Your thoughts close and your countenance loose" (literally 'open'), as George Herbert renders the saying in his collection of proverbs entitled *Jacula Prudentum* ('Shafts of the Wise').

In spite of the maxim Milton gave free expression to his strong Protestant views, offending the English Jesuits and others at Rome. See Mark Pattison's *Life of Milton*, pp. 33—38.

23. *Delphian oracle,* i.e. maxim which might have been uttered by the oracle of Apollo at Delphi.

35. *entertain you with home-novelties,* i.e. write news of events in England. No further correspondence between Sir Henry Wotton and Milton is extant.

COMUS.

G. = *Glossary.*

The performance. This took place on Michaelmas night, 1634, in the great Hall of Ludlow Castle, afterwards, says Professor Masson, called 'Comus Hall.' At the end of the room a stage was erected, concealed from the audience by a curtain or screen until the piece began. The Earl and Countess of Bridgewater occupied the Throne of State, the audience filling the rest of the hall. When everything was ready the scene, representing a wood, was disclosed.

THE PERSONS. The Masque contains six characters. We know how four of the parts were filled, viz. that the Lady was represented by the young Lady Alice Egerton, daughter of the Earl of Bridgewater; the two Brothers by her brothers Lord Brackley and Mr Thomas Egerton; and the Attendant Spirit by Lawes. It is likely that all four performers took part in the representation of *Arcades*, while it is known that Lord Brackley and his brother were among the Masquers in Carew's *Cælum Britannicum* acted in the previous February. Probably therefore *Comus* had the advantage of tolerably competent amateur acting. For Sabrina and Comus, no doubt, some relatives or friends of the Bridgewater family appeared.

presented, i.e. represented the characters. Cf. *The Tempest*, IV. 167, "when I presented Ceres"; and Tennyson's *Princess*, I.,

"Remembering how we three presented Maid,
    Or Nymph, or Goddess, at high tide of feast,
        In masque or pageant at my father's court."

The first Scene. The stage-directions throughout *Comus* are extremely simple. Usually Masque-writers—especially Ben Jonson, Campion, and Shirley—insert very full details as to the arrangement of the scenes, the dresses of the *dramatis personæ*, the music, and so forth.

discovers, reveals; see G.

The ATTENDANT SPIRIT *descends.* Probably the scenery in the background represented a hill; down this the Spirit comes, and at the actual representation of *Comus* his arrival was heralded by music. This we know from the *Bridgewater MS.* (the stage-copy in accordance with which the piece was performed), where the attendant Genius enters with a song. The song consisted of lines 976—1011.

To detach the passage from its context and make it a speech of arrival instead of departure only one slight change was necessary, viz. "*from* the heavens" in line 976 for "*to*." No doubt, Lawes made the change, and we may assume that the details of the performance of *Comus* were arranged by him, not Milton. By introducing music the alteration gave the piece a more effective opening from the stage point of view, but from the literary was objectionable. For having explained in the song that he came from heaven, it was superfluous for the Spirit to add that his mansion lay before the threshold of Jove's palace. Also, spoken as an Epilogue, the verses had a point which they here lose; they were meant to emphasize the moral of *Comus*.

1—9. This introductory speech serves as a prologue, of the type which Euripides employed so much as a way of explaining the purport of a play before any action took place. In the third draft of the scheme of *Paradise Lost*, which he originally intended to treat in the form of a tragedy, Milton gave the outline of a prologue similar to the present: "Moses προλογίζει, recounting how he assumed his true body; that it corrupts not" etc. Then followed a sketch of the drama, divided into five acts. The paper referred to is among the Milton MSS. at Trinity College; see *Introduction*, p. xxii.

2. *those.* Milton often uses the demonstrative, like Lat. *ille*, to mean 'the illustrious.' 'of whom all have heard.'

3. *spirits*, i.e. spiritual beings like himself, and the souls of the " just " (13).

insphered, dwelling in their allotted *sphere*. 'Sphere' is a word which he always uses with some reference to the Ptolemaic idea of the ten spheres or regions of space encircling the Earth, the supposed centre of the Universe. Cf. *Il Penseroso*, 88, 89,

> " unsphere
> The spirit of Plato,"

i.e. call it down from the sphere which it inhabits. So Shelley in the *Adonais* (XLVI.) represents the soul of Keats ascending upward and being welcomed by his brother-poets :

> " ' Thou art become as one of us,' they cry ;
> ' It was for thee yon kingless sphere has long
> Swung blind in an unascended majesty,
> Silent alone amid a Heaven of song.' "

4—11. What Milton has in mind is the classical conception of " the gods who live at ease " (*Par. Lost*, II. 868) in Olympus, the heaven of Greek mythology.

"Not by winds is it shaken, nor ever wet with rain, nor doth the snow come nigh thereto, but most clear air is spread about it cloudless, and the white light floats over it. Therein the blessed gods are glad for all their days," Homer, *Odyssey*, VI. 43—46 (Butcher and Lang's version). Cf. Tennyson's *Œnone* (which is full of Homeric spirit and allusion) :

> " gods, who have attain'd
> Rest in a happy place and quiet seats
> Above the thunder, with undying bliss."

serene ; scan *sérene* and see note on 273.

5. *smoke and stir ;* an echo perhaps of Horace's famous line *fumum et opes strepitumque Romæ* ('the reek and riches and din of Rome'), *Odes*, III. 29. 12. Note how "smoke" is antithetic to "serene" (used in the strict sense of Lat. *serenus*, bright, cloudless), and "stir" to "calm."

dim ; carrying on the picture in "smoke."

6. *low-thoughted care*, i.e. anxiety about the material interests of life. Pope borrowed the phrase ; cf. *Eloisa to Abelard*, 297, 298 :

> "O Grace serene ! O Virtue heavenly fair !
> Divine oblivion of low-thoughted care !"

7. i.e. penned up and shackled, like animals in a pound.

pestered...pinfold; see each in the Glossary.

8. *Strive to keep up;* implying that men do so *too long*, instead of being glad, when death comes, to change this life for a better.

frail, insecure, easily brought to an end, and full of unrest ("feverish") while it does last.

9. *the crown;* that is, the "incorruptible" crown (1 *Corinthians*, ix. 25) of everlasting life (*Revelation*, ii. 10, iii. 11).

10. *mortal change*, change from mortality. Some interpret 'a change brought about by his mortality.'

11. Cf. *Antony and Cleopatra*, I. 3. 28, "Though you in swearing shake the throned gods." Milton, however, is referring not only to this classical idea of the "quiet seats" of "the gods," but also to the Scriptural account of the "four and twenty seats" of the elders "clothed in white raiment; and [having] on their heads crowns of gold" (*Revelation*, iv. 4).

And here note a great feature of Milton's style, namely, the blending of Scriptural and classical associations. His mind was steeped in knowledge of the Bible and the classics, and what he writes is coloured now by one influence, now by the other, and often by both together in a way that seems to us sometimes quite incongruous. Thus in *Comus* and *Lycidas* we are moving in a pagan world where the deities of Greek and Latin mythology reign; nevertheless the Scriptural influence is often, if not always, present. This mixture of alien associations is opposed to modern taste.

the enthroned gods, i.e. the gods enthroned on. Such inversions of the order of words are common; cf. *Par. Lost*, I. 206, "With fixed anchor in his scaly rind." So in *Richard II.* III. 1, 9, "A happy gentleman in blood and lineaments." See Abbott's *Shakespearian Grammar*, p. 308.

12. *be;* see G. Abbott (p. 212) notes that *be* is often used "to refer to a number of persons, considered not individually, but as a kind or class"—as here.

13. *just*, righteous. *that golden key;* a favourite poetic allusion (see *Lyc.* 110, 111, note), variously applied. Ben Jonson in his Masque *The Barriers*, describing the figure of Truth, says :
"Her right hand holds a sun with burning rays,
Her left a curious bunch of golden keys
With which heaven's gates she locketh and displays."

Gray in the *Progress of Poesy* (III. 1) speaks of the Muse giving Shakespeare at his birth the "golden keys" of Comedy and Tragedy:

> "Thine too these golden keys, immortal Boy!
>   This can unlock the gates of Joy;
>   Of Horror that, and thrilling Fears,
>   Or ope the sacred source of sympathetic Tears."

And Tennyson speaks of the humble-born genius who rises to high place in the State, "And lives to clutch the golden keys" of office and power (*In Memoriam*, LXIV.). It is instructive to note how great imaginations give a fresh turn to the familiar, putting it in a new light, adding new associations.

15. *but for such*, except on their account, to benefit them.

16. *ambrosial*, heavenly, such as the gods have; see G.
weeds, raiment; see G.

17. The line is commonly explained 'the noisome exhalations of this sin-corrupted earth.' But *mould* has the general sense 'substance, material' in Milton (cf. 244), and I think that it is intended here—implying 'flesh,' the Spirit having assumed a mortal form. Cf. *Par. Lost*, IX. 485, where Adam is described as "Heroic built, though of *terrestrial mould*," which is explained by "formed of earth" (149), "this man of clay" (176).

18—21. For the division of empire cf. *Iliad*, XV. 190 et seq. where Poseidon (the Greek god of the sea=Latin Neptunus) says: "Three brethren are we, and sons of Kronos, whom Rhea bare, Zeus and myself, and Hades is the third, the ruler of the folk in the under-world. And in three lots are all things divided, and each drew a domain of his own, and to me fell the hoary sea, to be my habitation for ever, when we shook the lots: and Hades drew the murky darkness, and Zeus the wide heaven, in clear air and clouds, but the earth and the high Olympus are yet common to all—" *The Iliad, Done into English Prose* by Lang, Leaf and Myers.

19. *every...each*. A favourite variation with Milton; cf. 311 and *Lyc.* 93, 94. Etymologically *ever-y = ever-each*.

20. *Took in*, received as his share. *by lot;* cf. the extract just quoted from *Iliad*, XV. *'twixt;* referring to place, i.e. Neptune's realm lay between Heaven, the dominion of Jove (Gk. Zeus), and the nether world.

Some editors place a comma after *took in*, and explain *by lot 'twixt*=by agreement between.

nether Jove; that is Hades (Lat. Pluto), often called 'the infernal Zeus' (καταχθόνιος, literally 'underground,' hence 'belonging to the lower regions').

21—23. Newton thought that the germ of this was Gaunt's famous description of England as "This precious stone set in the silver sea," *Richard II.* II. 1. 46. Probably the whole passage was in Milton's mind when he wrote the lines 21—28.

23. *unadorned*, i.e. without other adornment.

24, 25. i.e. Neptune entrusts each island to the government of some particular sea-deity—these inferior rulers all acknowledging him as their supreme lord.

27. *little*, i.e. as compared with the great trident, a threepronged (Lat. *tridens*) sceptre, of Neptune. Spenser in the dedicatory stanzas of *The Faerie Queene* salutes Elizabeth as "Great Ladie of the greatest Isle."

29. *quarters*, assigns. *blue-haired.* From the stage-directions in other Masques it may be inferred that convention associated hair of this hue with water-deities. It was intended, of course, to symbolise the colour of the waves. Thus in Beaumont and Fletcher's *Masque of the Inner Temple and Gray's Inn* (1612) four Naiads appear on the stage, "with blueish tresses on their heads, garlands of water-lilies." Poetic tradition counts for much in the Masque.

Masson says: "There seems to be some emphasis on the phrase 'blue-haired deities,' as if these were a special section of the 'tributary gods' of line 24. Can there be a recollection of 'blue' as the British colour, inherited from the old times of the blue-stained Britons who fought with Cæsar?"

30. *this tract;* Wales.

31. *noble Peer*, i.e. the Earl of Bridgewater, who was present. Milton in the course of *Comus* pays a compliment to all those who were mainly concerned in the performance of the Masque; cf. 86—88, 244—248, 297—301, 494—496. Personal and flattering allusion of this kind was a marked feature of Masques.

It was no unusual thing for the Elizabethan dramatists to insert pieces of flattery to the Queen when they knew that she would be present at the representation of a play.

mickle, great; see G.

32. *with tempered awe*, with a due mixture of firmness and conciliation. It is said that the new Lord President received particular instructions as to the official course which he should pursue.

33. *nation*, i.e. the Welsh. Milton knew that there would be Welshmen present among his audience. One of Ben Jonson's *Entertainments* fulfils the promise of its title—*For the Honour of Wales*—and pays every possible compliment to the "old and haughty nation, proud in arms."

34. *nursed in princely lore.* "In this phrase some find an allusion to a link with Royalty at a remote point in the pedigree of the Egerton family; others find a reference to the fact that the young people had been a good deal at Court. The more natural meaning, however, is simply 'highly-educated'"—*Masson.*

36. *new-intrusted.* The Earl's appointment dated from the summer of 1631; but he did not formally take up his duties till 1634.

37. *perplexed*, entangled; the Latin sense, as in *Par. Lost*, IV. 176. Cf. Pope, *Messiah*, 73, "Waste sandy valleys, once perplexed with thorn."

38. *horror*, awe-inspiring appearance.

41. Cf. *Arcades*, 44, 45, where the Genius of the Wood proclaims himself the minister of Jove.

43. *I will tell you.* Johnson condemned this address to the audience; "a mode of communication so contrary to the nature of dramatic representation, that no precedents can support it." But *Comus* is a Masque, and a Masque must not be judged in the same way as an ordinary drama.

43—45. A claim to novelty of theme or treatment is one of the conventions of poetry influenced by the classics. Thus at the outset (I. 16) of *Par. Lost* Milton says that his Muse is about to essay "Things unattempted yet in prose or rhyme." Cf. Horace's *carmina non prius audita...canto* ('I sing strains never heard before'), *Odes*, III. 1. 2—4, and IV. 9. 3, 4, where Horace claims for himself the merit of originality of style.

44, 45. Milton has in mind a scene such as Scott depicts in *The Lay of the Last Minstrel.* Some have argued that these "bards" of the middle ages were "honoured guests in the castles of the nobles" to whose service they were attached; others that they were "merely wandering harpers." Perhaps some belonged to the one class, some to the other; until minstrelsy fell upon evil days, and of each of its latest few followers it could be said:

> "A wandering Harper, scorn'd and poor,
>
> He begg'd his bread from door to door,
>
> And tuned, to please a peasant's ear,
>
> The harp a king had loved to hear."

hall or bower. A traditional phrase; cf. Spenser's *Astrophel,* 27, 28:

> "And he himselfe seemed made for meriment,
>
> Merily masking both in bowre and hall."

"Hall" = the room of State in which the whole household assembled; "bower" = the ladies' private room. Cf. *The Lay of the Last Minstrel,* Canto I. 1, 11; and Wordsworth's Sonnet "Milton, thou shouldst be living."

48. The allusion is to the story of Bacchus, the god of wine, being seized on his way from Icaria to Naxos. "He hired a ship which belonged to *Tyrrhenian* [cf. 49] pirates; but the men, instead of landing at Naxos, steered towards Asia, to sell him there as a slave. Thereupon the god changed the mast and oars into serpents, and himself into a lion; ivy grew round the vessel, and the sound of flutes was heard on every side; the sailors were seized with madness, leaped into the sea, and were *metamorphosed into dolphins*"—Smith's *Classical Dictionary.*

After the mariners transformed; a Latinism (*post nautas mutatos*) such as we get in phrases like *post conditam urbem* ('since the foundation of the city'), where the participle, as it were, does the duty of a noun followed by a genitive case. Milton uses this idiom with 'after' and 'since'; cf. *Par. Lost,* I. 573, "since created Man," i.e. since the creation of.

49. *the Tyrrhene shore,* the coast of Etruria which, roughly speaking, was the same region as the modern Tuscany (cf. "Tuscan" in 48). *listed,* pleased; see G.

50. *Circe*; a famous sorceress, described by Homer in *Odyssey,* X., who dwelt on the island of Aea, off the western coast of Italy; daughter of the Sun-god and Perse, one of the daughters of the Ocean. On his wanderings after the Trojan war Odysseus visited her with his companions, some of whom she changed by her magic draughts into animals. By the help of the god Hermes (see 636, 637) Odysseus was able to resist

her enchantments and make her change his companions back again into men. Homer's description has this peculiar interest in the history of literature, that it became the model of all the accounts of fair enchantresses dwelling in palaces which we get in Tasso and Spenser and other writers of romance.

"The bringing of Bacchus to Circe's Island is Milton's own invention, with a view to the parentage he had resolved on for Comus"—*Masson*. The fact is that Milton sometimes *makes his own mythology*.

fell, chanced, came upon, in his voyage.

Who knows not Circe? The repetition of a name or word in the form of a question was a favourite artifice, especially with Spenser. Cf. *The Shepheards Calender*, August:

"A doolefull verse

Of Rosalend (who knows not Rosalend?)."

It is one of the imitations of archaic manner in Matthew Arnold's *Thyrsis*; cf. "I know these slopes; who knows them if not I?"

52, 53. There seems to be the underlying thought that physical uprightness symbolises moral. The poet was himself a very graceful man. Aubrey tells us, "his harmonical and ingenious soul dwelt in a beautiful and well proportioned body."

54. *This nymph*, i.e. Circe.

55. The representations of Bacchus in art differ widely, but the youthful god described here is a recognised type; cf. Dryden's poem *Alexander's Feast*. It was probably the traditional association of ivy with the wine-god that led to the custom of affixing an ivy-bush at the doors of taverns: whence the proverb "good wine needs no bush"; cf. *As You Like It*, *Epilogue*, 4. 6.

56. *parted*; cf. French *partir*, to depart.

57. Comus typifies sensuality, as his name implies, and magical power. In the scene with the Lady (659—813) he represents sensual pleasure. To the Attendant Spirit he appears rather as "a sorcerer" (521), "that damned wizard" (571), "the foul enchanter" (645). Cf. "but [like] his mother *more*." He owes the one character to his father the wine-god; the other to his mother the sorceress, skilled in magic drugs (πολυφάρμακος, as Homer calls her, *Odyssey*, x. 276). The parentage, as we saw, is Milton's own invention; nothing could be more appropriate.

59. *frolic*. German *fröhlich*, 'gay.'

60. i.e. France and Spain. Cf. *Par. Lost*, I. 520, 521:

"Fled over Adria to the Hesperian fields,

And o'er the Celtic roamed the utmost isles."

Iberia ; a classical name for Spain.

61. *this;* pointing to the scenery representing a wood. *ominous;* not so much 'threatening,' as 'full of portents or magical appearances.' The wood is peopled with "calling shapes, and beckoning shadows dire," 207. *Ominous* is a dissyllable = *om'nous*.

65. *orient,* bright, lustrous (as described in 673); see G.

66. *the drouth of,* the thirst caused by the sun.

67. *fond,* foolish; see G. The epithet is transferred to the thirst from the thirsty man who indulges it foolishly.

69. An echo of *Genesis* i. 27: "So God created man in his own image, in the image of God created he him"; and *Hebrews* i. 3, "the express image of his person." *express,* exact.

71. *ounce.* Also written *once ;* it is a kind of lynx—*felis uncia.* Perhaps from Persian *yúz* (nasalised), a panther, lynx.

72. A departure from Homer's account, which represents Circe's victims as changed entirely into beasts. Newton notes that this partial metamorphosis suited better the purposes of the stage. Each character would wear a mask representing some animal's head, as does Bottom in *A Midsummer-Night's Dream.* Cf. the stage-direction that follows—"headed like sundry sorts of wild beasts, but otherwise like men and women."

73. *perfect,* complete; from completeness comes the idea 'excellence.' French *parfait.*

74. Milton has not followed Homer strictly; cf. *Odyssey,* X. 237 et seq.: "Now when Circe had given them the cup and they had drunk it off, presently she smote them with a wand, and in the styes of the swine she penned them. So they had the head and voice, the bristles and the shape of swine, *but their mind abode even as of old.* Thus were they penned there weeping"—Butcher and Lang's translation (as in the next note). Perhaps Homer's account gives greater pathos: Circe's victims are conscious of the contrast between their present and past; and pathos is largely a matter of self-appreciated contrast. Milton's account emphasizes the completeness of the power of Comus, i.e. the deadliness of the pleasure he has to offer.

76. Cf. *Odyssey,* X. 235, 236: "and Circe mixed harmful

drugs with the food to make them [her victims] utterly forget
their own country." The lotus-flower possessed this peculiar
power, and Milton, no doubt, has in mind the description of
the 'lotus-eaters' (Lotophagi) who dwelt on an island off the
Mediterranean coast of Africa, and offered the lotus to all
strangers : and "whosoever of them did eat the honey-sweet
fruit of the lotus, had no more wish to come back, but there
he chose to abide with the lotus-eating men, ever feeding on the
lotus, and forgetful of his homeward way"—*Odyssey*, IX. 94—97.

See Tennyson's poem *The Lotos-Eaters*, in which the rhythm
and alliteration and verbal effects convey an exquisite sense of
listless languid bliss. And turn to the witty 'perversion' of the
present passage in the *Dunciad*, IV, where Pope makes the high-
priest of Dullness offer to her victims "the cup which causes a
total oblivion of all obligations," so that (for example) the
man who has won Court-favour quite ignores his past :

> "a wizard old his cup extends,
> Which whoso tastes forgets his former friends,
> Sire, ancestors, himself."

79. *adventurous*; where you are likely to meet with adven-
tures; 'dangerous'.

80. The simile is repeated in *Par. Lost*, I. 745, 746. There,
as here, the rhythm of the verses suggests the motion described.

81. *convoy*, escort. Low Lat. *conviare*, to bring on the
way (Lat. *via*). The same word as *convey*.

83. i.e. robes dyed in the tints of the rainbow; Iris being
the goddess of the rainbow and "many-colour'd messenger" of
Juno, *Tempest*, IV. 76. See *Par. Lost*, XI. 244.

85. Alluding to Lawes's connection, as music-master, with
the family of the Earl of Bridgewater. So in 493.

86—88. The compliment to Lawes is repeated at 494—496.
Milton chooses his epithets, "soft," "smooth-dittied," with
careful reference to the qualities of Lawes's music. See p. 40.

87. *Knows to*. For the construction (where we should
insert *how*) cf. *Lyc*. 10, 11. The idiom is an obvious classicism,
on the model of the infinitive after words like ἐπίσταμαι, *calleo*.

87, 88. Note Milton's favourite form of alliteration, *w...w*,
corresponding to the alliterative use of *v* in Latin poetry. Cf.
Lyc. 13, and compounds like 'wide-wasting' (*Par. Lost*, VI. 253),
'wide-waving' (*Par. Lost*, XI. 121), 'wide-watered' (*Il Pen*. 75).

88. *nor of less faith,* i.e. "not less trustworthy than he is skilled in music"—*Masson.*

90. *Likeliest,* most fitting; so in *2 Henry IV.* III. 2. 273: "They are your likeliest men, and I would have you served with the best." Not far removed from *likely*=pleasing; as we say, 'a likely lad.'

91, 92. i.e. nearest at hand to lend the help that this occasion requires.

92. *Viewless,* invisible. Cf. *The Passion,* 50. Milton remembered Claudio's "viewless winds," *Measure for Measure,* III. 1. 124. The termination *less* is now active, and *viewless* in modern E. would mean 'having no view.' But in the English of Shakespeare and Milton the force of adjectival and participial endings is not stereotyped.

The Attendant Spirit moves from the stage, and Comus appears with his followers. Strictly this was the Anti-masque, or comic interlude, and probably would have been treated as such at greater length by Ben Jonson.

Stage-direction. The stage-direction in the *Cambridge MS.* omits several points here introduced: e.g. there is no mention of torches, which would add greatly to the effectiveness of the scene, nor have the characters "glistering" apparel. When Milton wrote *Comus* he thought chiefly of the poetry and the moral which it enforced; mere scenic details could be left to Lawes, who had been so busy earlier in the year over the production of Shirley's *Triumph of Peace* and Carew's *Cælum Britannicum.*

Comus would wear a fantastic dress to remind the audience of his supernatural powers; cf. the allusion in line 157 to his "quaint habits." Campion in one of his Masques brings "two enchanters" on the stage—Rumour and Error; the latter dressed "in a skin coat scaled like a serpent, and an antic habit painted with snakes, a hair of curled snakes, and a deformed Vizard"— Bullen's *Campion,* p. 216. Symbolical garb of this kind was much employed, Masques dealing so often with allegory.

his glass; containing his magic potion; cf. 65. *rout,* band.

glistering. Referring, probably, to the cloth of silver and tinsel (see 877), which was used a good deal on the stage.

93. *The star,* the evening-star; "thy folding-star," says Collins in his *Ode to Evening.* Keightley notes that Milton has adapted Shakespeare's converse description of the morning-star,

Measure for Measure, IV. 2. 218, "Look, the unfolding star calls up the shepherd." In the one case the star is Hesperus; in the other, Phosphorus ('the Light-bringer'); cf. Tennyson's *In Memoriam*, CXXI:

> "Sweet Hesper-Phosphor, double name
> For what is one, the first, the last."

95—97. Some think that Milton refers to the classical belief that the waves of the Atlantic hissed as the fiery wheels of the setting sun's chariot touched them.

96. *allay*, steep, cool.

97. *steep*. Standing on the sea-shore we can verify the accuracy of *steep*. Tennyson gives us the same picture in *The Progress of Spring*, VI., "The slant seas leaning on the mangrove copse." Some interpret 'deep,' like Latin *altus*.

stream; alluding, perhaps, to the Homeric conception of the Ocean as a great river surrounding the earth.

98. *slope*, sinking in the horizon. The whole picture in 98, 99 is amplified in *Par. Lost*, IV. 539—543.

101. The imagery of *Psalm* XIX. 5, "In them hath he set a tabernacle for the sun: which cometh forth as a bridegroom out of his chamber" (Prayer-Book).

105. *rosy twine*, twined roses. An allusion to the classical custom of weaving chaplets of flowers, especially roses, at entertainments, and perfuming the hair with unguents.

106. i.e. diffusing fragrance and moist with wine.

107. *Rigour*. *Comus* has many of these personified abstractions. The use of them is a characteristic of Milton's early style; cf. the *Nativity Ode, L' Allegro, Il Penseroso*. In 18th century poetry, e.g. in Gray and Collins, this rather tricky artifice became a mannerism. It was an aspect of the "poetical diction" which Wordsworth denounced in the famous preface to the *Lyrical Ballads*. Usually the noun is accompanied by an adjective—e.g. "pure-eyed Faith."

The influence of the old Morality-plays (which affected the Elizabethan drama much, especially upon its ethical side), and of the Masque itself, had fostered this method of personification, so common in Latin writers.

110. *saws*, maxims. The Justice in *As You Like It*, II. 7. 156, is "full of wise saws." *Saw, say, saga* (Icelandic) are allied.

111. *fire*. Alluding to the old theory that everything is

composed of **four** elements—earth, water, fire and air: the two last being the lighter elements. "I am fire and air," says Cleopatra (*Antony and Cleopatra*, v. 2. 292), about to die: henceforth she will be free of the substance that clogs her spirit.

113. Cf. "the spheres of watchful fire," *Vacation Exercise*, 40.

114. Milton is fond of likening the motions of the heavenly bodies to a dance; cf. "lead" and perhaps "round"=round dance (see **144**), though 'circle, revolution' would also suit. Thus he speaks of the "mystic dance" of the planets, *Par. Lost*, v. 178 (and see also 620—624).

the months and years. Cf. *Par. Lost*, VII. 339—342 (echoing the words of *Genesis* i. 14).

115. *sounds*, straits of sea; see G.

116. *to*, in obedience to,—referring to the influence of the moon on the tides; or perhaps 'to the accompaniment of,' i.e. under the light of.

wavering morrice, i.e. an undulating dance; cf. Keats's *Endymion*, IV., where the four Seasons join in a "floating morris." Another name was *Morisco*, i.e. *Moorish* dance. It is said to have been introduced into England in the reign of Edward III. when John of Gaunt returned from Spain. A morris (the more usual spelling) formed, and in some counties still forms, part of the rustic festivities at Whitsuntide and May-day; cf. *Henry V.* II. 4. 25, "busied with a Whitsun morris-dance"; and *All's Well That Ends Well*, II. 2. 25, "As fit as...a morris for May-day."

117. *tawny*. He wrote *yellow*, and perhaps changed to avoid too obvious comparison with Ariel's song "Come unto these yellow sands," *Tempest*, I. 2. 376. The nymph in *Endymion*, II. ruled over "grotto-sands tawny and gold." The influence of Milton's diction is very marked in Keats's poems.

shelves, banks of streams.

118. *pert*, lively, alert. See the Glossary for *pert, faery*.

121. *wakes*. Properly a *wake*="the feast of the dedication of a church, formerly kept by watching [i.e. keeping *awake*] all night"—*Schmidt:* hence any merry-making kept up late.

127. *dun;* cf. "the dun air," i.e. dusky, of Chaos, *Par. Lost*, III. 72.

122. Comus celebrates the night time in his twofold character of magician and patron of license.

Gray's *Ode* written for the installation of the Duke of Grafton as Chancellor of Cambridge University begins rather curiously:

> "Hence! Avaunt! ('tis holy ground)
> Comus and his midnight crew."

128—130. *Cotytto*, or Cotys, a Thracian goddess. The Cotyttia, a festival held in her honour, took place at night. These licentious rites were secret; Juvenal (*Satire* II. 91, 92) speaks of their being celebrated with "secret torch" (*secreta tæda*).

131. *ne'er called but when*, i.e. only invoked at night.

dragon. Newton considers this an allusion to the idea that the chariot of the night was drawn by dragons; cf. *Cymbeline*, II. 2. 48, "Swift, swift, you dragons of the night!" *Dragons*, i.e. serpents, were chosen because of their proverbial sharpness of sight, the word (Gk. δράκων) coming from a root 'to see.'

132. *Stygian darkness*, i.e. darkness as of the nether world. "Abhorred Styx, the flood of deadly hate" (*Par. Lost*, II. 577), one of the four rivers of Hades, is a synonym of hell. From Gk. στυγεῖν, 'to hate.'

spets; an obsolete form of *spits.* In *The Merchant of Venice*, I. 3. 113, the Quartos and the 1st Folio have "And spet upon my Jewish gaberdine," changed in modern texts to *spit.*

134. *cloudy*, wrapt in clouds. *ebon*, black as ebony.

135. *Hecate;* the goddess of sorcery and witchcraft and mysterious midnight "rites" (535), as in *Macbeth*, where she is the patroness of the Witches. Scan *Hecat'*, as the original editions read. The scansion is very common; cf. Byron, *Childe Harold*, II. 22, "Alike beheld beneath pale Hecate's blaze."

138—141. These lines are a little mosaic of Shakespearian touches. Cf. *2 Henry VI.* IV. 1. 1, "The gaudy, blabbing and remorseful day"; a passage (written by Marlowe, I believe, not Shakespeare), upon which Milton draws later (552, 553). For *Indian steep*, see 139 note; for *tell-tale* cf. *Lucrece*, 806, "Make me not object to the tell-tale Day."

139. *nice*, squeamish. Comus sneers at the Morn as too prudish to approve of their rites. See G.

the Indian steep. Cf. *A Midsummer-Night's Dream*, II. 1. 69, "the farthest steep of India" (Folio reading).

Indian, i.e. eastern.

141. *descry*, reveal; as in *The Faerie Queene*, VI. 7. 12.

144. *round*, a country-dance, the favourite one being Sellenger's (St Leger's) Round. Titania invited Oberon to join their round—*A Midsummer-Night's Dream*, II. I. 140. For the epithets cf. *L' Allegro*, 34, " On the light fantastic toe."

The Measure. " Measure denoted any dance remarkable for its well-defined rhythm, but in time the name was applied to a solemn and stately dance of the nature of a Pavan or a Minuet. The dignified character of the dance is proved by the use of the expression to 'tread a measure'; a phrase of frequent occurrence in the works of the Elizabethan dramatists. It is somewhat remarkable that no trace can be found of any special music to which Measures were danced; this circumstance seems to prove that there was no definite form of dance tune for them, but that any stately and rhythmical air was used for the purpose "—Grove's *Dictionary of Music. Measure*, however, came to be applied to any sort of dance, and the stage-direction in the *Cambridge MS.* describes the dance here intended as "wild and rude."

145. *Break off*, i.e. cease dancing. This is the "stop of sudden silence" mentioned in 552.

147. *shrouds*, places of shelter; see G.

151. *trains*, allurements; see G.

152, 153. Cf. the notes on 50 and 74. The *Cambridge MS.* adds the direction *They all scatter*.

154. *dazzling*. The *Cambridge MS.* has *powdered;* cf. "magic dust," 165. No doubt as the actor spoke these lines, 153—156 (cf. "Thus"), he scattered some powder in the air. A coloured light too may have been burnt behind the scene to heighten the effect—*Masson*.

spongy, because it seems, like a sponge, to drink in and retain the spells; cf. *Troilus and Cressida*, II. 2. 12, "More spongy to suck in the sense of fear."

155. *blear*, deceptive. To *blear* the eyes is to *blur*, i.e. make them dim. Dimness led easily to the notion of deceiving.

156. *presentments*. Cf. Hamlet's "counterfeit presentment," where 'representation,' 'picture' is the sense required, III. 4. 54.

157. *quaint habits*, i.e. his fanciful magician's dress. Milton has to explain why Comus at his next entry (244) appears as a "gentle shepherd" (271).

160. *ends*, purposes, intentions.

161. *glozing*, flattering; with the idea of falsehood. See G.

162. *not unplausible*, i.e. *very* specious; an instance of the figure of speech called *meiosis* (Gk. μείωσις, 'diminution'), by which you express in *very* moderate language something which you really wish to emphasise, e.g., 'it is no small pleasure to'=it is a very great pleasure to. Another name for this figure of rhetoric is *litotes* ('simplicity,' from the Greek).

163. *Wind me*, i.e. obtain his confidence. Needlessly changed in some editions to *win*. Shakespeare has *wind* with the sense 'to get an unfair advantage over'; e.g. in *King Lear*, I. 2. 106, "seek him out: wind me into him, I pray you."

the easy-hearted man, unsuspicious people.

165. *virtue*, peculiar power; cf. *virtuous*, 621; see G.

167. *gear*, business. Properly *gear*='apparatus,' 'tackle,' as in compounds, *travelling* or *fishing gear*, etc. In Elizabethan English it usually has the wider meaning of 'affair,' 'matter in hand.' Cf. *Romeo and Juliet*, II. 4. 107, "Here's goodly gear," i.e. as we might say colloquially, 'a pretty business.'

166—169. The edition of 1673 differs from that of 1645, by omitting 167, transposing 168, 169, and giving *hear* for *here* in 169. Most editors keep to the text of the earlier edition, except that they substitute *hear* for *here*. Some, however, follow the 1645 ed. in printing "And hearken, if I may, her business *here*," and take *hearken* transitively.

168. *fairly*, softly; cf. "Soft and fair, friar," *Much Ado About Nothing*, V. 4. 72. Comus steps back into the wood.

172. *ill-managed*, disorderly.

173—177. Milton is thinking of a shearing feast and harvest-home, such as Herrick describes in the *Hesperides* (a work from which we learn much about the rural life of Milton's generation). See again 848, *Lyc.* 117, and *L' Allegro*, 91—114.

174. *hinds*, peasants; see G.

175. *granges*, barns, granaries; from Lat. *granum*, corn. Now a poetic word in this sense; cf. Tennyson's *Demeter*, "Rejoicing in the harvest and the grange."

177. *amiss*, i.e. in a wrong way.

178. *swilled*, drunken; a coarse word, applicable to animals but suiting the context here. Cf. the description in *Par. Lost*, I. 502, of revellers "flown with insolence and wine," i.e. flushed with.

179. *wassailers;* see G.

180. *inform,* find guidance for. Cf. *Samson Agonistes,* 335.

181. *blind,* obscure; as in 'blind alley.'

183. *to lodge,* to pass the night.

184. *the spreading favour,* the kindly shelter.

188. *then when;* a favourite emphatic phrase with Milton; cf. *Par. Lost,* IV. 970, "Then, when I am thy captive, talk of chains."

gray-hooded Even; hence Keats's line in *Endymion,* I. :

"She sings but to her love, nor e'er conceives
    How tiptoe Night holds back her dark-gray hood."

189. *sad,* sober, serious, without any notion of sorrow; cf. *sadly* in line 509, and see G.

votarist. Used of anyone who had taken a vow (*votum*); here a vow of pilgrimage. Cf. *Timon of Athens,* IV. 3. 27, "I am no idle votarist."

A *palmer* was "one who bore a palm-branch in memory of having been to the Holy Land"—*Skeat.*

The comparison between "the *gray*-hooded Even" and a palmer may be illustrated by one of Greene's lyrics describing Love dressed as a pilgrim :

"Down the valley gan he track,
    Bag and bottle at his back,
    In a surcoat all of gray ;
    Such wear palmers on the way,
    When with scrip and staff they see
    Jesus' grave on Calvary."

So Collins in his *Ode,* "How sleep the brave," stanza 2 :

"There Honour comes, a pilgrim gray,
    To bless the turf that wraps their clay."

190. i.e. they left her just as the sun was sinking.

193. *engaged,* ventured, committed.

195—225. From "else O thievish Night" down to "tufted grove" (225) is omitted in the *Bridgewater MS.,* i.e. was not acted ; perhaps to lighten the part of the young lady ; perhaps from motives of delicacy—*Masson.*

195—200. This piece of imagery has been very generally censured as far-fetched and unnatural. The fact is that Milton's early poems do show just a trace of the fault which mars the works of those fantastic contemporary writers, such as Donne and

Crashaw, whom Johnson calls the 'metaphysical' poets (*Life* of Cowley). One of the 'notes of this school of writers was the use of fantastic imagery, far-fetched metaphors. Cf. the *Nativity Ode*, 229—231 :

> "So when the sun *in bed*,
> *Curtained* with cloudy red,
> *Pillows* his chin upon an orient wave."

The image there is a mere 'conceit,' which barely escapes the grotesque.

198.　*their lamps;* a much used comparison ; cf. Shelley's line, "The lamps of Heaven flash with a softer light," *Adonais*, XIX. Shakespeare quaintly compared the stars to candles in *Romeo and Juliet*, III. 5. 9—"Night's candles are burnt out"; and *Macbeth*, II. 1. 5.

203.　*perfect in*, perfectly clear to.

204.　*single*, total.

205.　*what might*? what *could* this be? The original sense of *may* was 'can,' 'be able.'

207—209. Milton was drawing upon popular superstition. Perhaps some of his audience believed in these "calling shapes" and "airy tongues" of which medieval romance is full. Editors cite many illustrations, e.g. the "strange shapes" and "sounds and sweet airs" and "voices" of *The Tempest*, III. 2. 144—149, 3. 18—39.

207.　*beckoning shadows dire*. The order (Greek) of the words—a noun placed between two qualifying words—is a favourite with Milton. Chaucer too has it. In his note on *Lycidas*, 6, Mr Jerram quotes Euripides, *Phœnissæ*, 234, νιφόβολον ὄρος ἱρόν ('snowclad mount divine,' viz. Parnassus). Gray probably borrowed the device from Milton ; cf. his *Elegy*, 53, "Full many a gem of purest ray serene." Cf. also Tennyson's early poems, in which the influence of Milton is very noticeable ; e.g. *The Lotos-Eaters*, VII., "With half-dropt eyelid still," and *The Palace of Art*, "In diverse raiment strange."

beckoning. Like the ghost in *Hamlet*, I. 4. 58.

208.　*airy tongues*. Cf. *Endymion*, IV.:

> "No, never more
> Shall airy voices cheat me to the shore."

Probably due to *Comus*. *syllable*, i.e. pronounce clearly.

212.　*siding*, going by the side; hence 'defending.'

214. *girt with golden wings.* Possibly a reminiscence of *Psalm* lxviii. 13: "yet shall ye be as the wings of a dove covered with silver, and her feathers with yellow gold."

215. *unblemished,* that may not be blemished; see 349, note.

Chastity. A departure from the ordinary Trinity of Faith, Hope and Charity (to keep the Authorised Version of ἀγάπη). *Comus* is an enforcement of the doctrine intensely sacred in Milton's eye—the doctrine of purity; and it is worth noting that the substantive *chastity* occurs seven times in the poem; the adjective *chaste* four times.

216. *ye;* the original distinction between *ye* (nominative) and *you* (objective) was often ignored by Elizabethan writers; we see it in *John* xv. 16, "Ye have not chosen me, but I have chosen you."

217. *Supreme.* Scan *súpreme;* see note on 273. The sense in 217—219 is: 'he who uses all evil powers as agents to execute his displeasure against wicked men would send...'

221. *Was I deceived?* A moment before she had expressed the belief that Providence would, if necessary, interpose to protect her. The rift in the clouds seems an omen: the moonlight is like a "glistering guardian."

223, 224. Milton employs sparingly, but with fine effect, the artifice of verbal repetition. Cf. *Par. Lost*, VII. 25, 26:

> "though fallen on evil days,
> On evil days though fallen, and evil tongues."

No modern poet uses this device more beautifully than Tennyson. Cf. in *Enoch Arden* the latter part of the great passage that begins "The mountain wooded to the peak."

224. Cf. the proverb "no cloud without a silver lining."

225. *casts.* We should expect *cast* after *does* in 223.

228. *new-enlivened,* i.e. by the favourable sign in the sky.

230. Invocations of Echo, whose reply would be counterfeited behind the scenery, were not uncommon in Masques. It was a pretty, fanciful device appropriate to the fanciful character of the ordinary Masque. Also, it gave an opportunity for the introduction of Music (ever a great feature of Masque-performances).

Echo, a mountain-nymph (Oread, from ὄρος, a mountain) who was changed by Juno into an Echo—"that is, a being with no control over its tongue, which is neither able to speak before anybody else has spoken, nor to be silent when somebody else has spoken. Echo in this state fell desperately in love with Narcissus; but as her love was not returned, she pined away in grief, so that in the end there remained of her nothing but her voice"—*Classical Dictionary*.

231. *airy shell;* some interpret 'the vault of Heaven'= "sphere," 241; others 'a shell with air in it,' lying by the river's side (232).

232. There is said to be no classical authority for this association of Echo and Meander, though we meet with it in Gray's *Progress of Poesy*, 69—72, a reminiscence perhaps of the present passage. It has been suggested, however, that the mention of the Meander in poetry is due to the fact that it was a special resort of the swan, which, like the nightingale, is one of the favourite birds of poets; cf. the legend of the 'swan's song.' Meander is the modern Mendereh, rising in Phrygia. The circuitous course of the river has given us the word *meander*.

241. *Parley*, conversation, dialogue; since an echo seems to keep up a dialogue with the voice.

Daughter of the sphere. Cf. the epithet 'sphere-born' applied to the "harmonious sisters, Voice and Verse," *At a Solemn Music*, 2. There is perhaps an allusion to the notion of "the music of the spheres," which is referred to in 1021; see note there.

242. *translated*, raised aloft.

243. i.e. re-echo the music of heaven. Note that the verse is an Alexandrine (six feet), the only one in the poem. Milton was fond of the metre; see the *Nativity Ode*, or *Death of a Fair Infant*. An Alexandrine rounds off effectively the close of a stanza; cf. the *Odes* of Gray and Collins. The abuse of the artifice excited Pope's ridicule, *Essay on Criticism*, 356, 357:
"A needless Alexandrine ends the song,
  That, like a wounded snake, drags its slow length along."

244. In the *Cambridge MS.* the return of Comus to the scene is marked by a stage-direction—*Comus looks in and speaks.* Probably he appears at the side of the stage, not revealing himself to the Lady till 265.

244, 245. The language of the couplet is a little extravagant; but we must remember that it was inserted out of compliment to the composer and the Lady Egerton who had sung the air.

246—248. Probably a reference to the idea, attributed to Pythagoras, that the soul *is* a harmony. Plato in the *Phædo* compares it to a harmony. Cf. *The Merchant of Venice*, v. 63, where Farmer quoted Hooker's *Ecclesiastical Polity*, Bk. v. "Touching musical harmony...so pleasing effects it hath in that very part of man which is most divine, that some have been thereby induced to think, that the soul itself by nature is or hath in it harmony."

247. *moves the vocal air*, fills the air till it becomes vocal (a *proleptic* use of the epithet).

248. *To*, so as to. *his*, its; see G.

249, 250. "Even silence herself was content to convey her mortal enemy, sound, on her wings, so greatly was she charmed with its harmony"—*Warburton*.

251, 252. These lines exemplify Milton's faculty for suggesting by means of metaphor—the quality in which Coleridge among modern poets is eminent. We are to conceive of darkness as being a dusky bird whose ruffled wings cover the earth—imagery which is illustrated by *L'Allegro*, 6, where "brooding Darkness spreads his jealous wings." And on this bird of night falls the spell of harmony, just as in the first Pythian Ode of Pindar the eagle of Zeus was charmed to rest by music; cf. Gray, *The Progress of Poesy*, I. 2:

> "Perching on the sceptred hand
> Of Jove, thy magic lulls the feather'd king
> With ruffled plumes, and flagging wing:
> Quench'd in dark clouds of slumber lie
> The terror of his beak, and light'ning of his eye."

The raven is chosen as symbolising darkness by its colour. Mrs Gaskell has a happy allusion to this passage: "she was late —that she knew she would be. Miss Simmonds was vexed and cross. That also she had anticipated—and had intended to smooth her raven down by extraordinary diligence"—*Mary Barton*, II. p. 27. Cf. too *In Memoriam*, "Let darkness keep her raven gloss."

251. *fall*, cadence; cf. "That strain again! it had a dying fall," *Twelfth Night*, I. i. 4. Cf. *close* in 548.

253. *the Sirens;* "sea-nymphs who had the power of charming by their songs all who heard them...According to Homer, the island of the Sirens was situated between Aea

[Circe's isle] and the rock of Scylla [cf. 257], near the S.W. coast of Italy"—*Classical Dictionary*. Strictly the Sirens (Homer says there were two) had nothing to do with Circe.

254. In *Odyssey*, X. 350, 351, Circe is waited upon by four maidens, "born of the wells and of the woods and of the holy rivers, that flow forward into the salt sea." The Naiads were "the nymphs of fresh water, whether of rivers, lakes, brooks, or springs"—*Classical Dictionary*: hence their association with wild-flowers. Cf. *Par. Regained*, II. 355, 356.

flowery-kirtled; "dressed with garlands of flowers for skirts" —*Dr Bradshaw*. Or perhaps, 'flower-decked.'

255. *potent herbs*. Cf. *Æneid*, VII. 19, 20, where Vergil speaks of the victims whom "the cruel goddess Circe had transformed from men into beasts *potentibus herbis*."

256. *prisoned*, i.e. in the body; cf. 385.

257. *lap it in Elysium*, fill it with an intense bliss.

Elysium; the Paradise of Greek mythology; hence a synonym of supreme happiness.

257—259. Homer makes Odysseus sail some distance beyond the island of the Sirens, and out of reach of their song, before he came to Scylla and Charybdis. All through this passage Milton adapts rather than follows Homer's account of the classical figures enumerated.

"*Scylla* and *Charybdis*, the names of two rocks between Italy and Sicily, and only a short distance from one another. In the one of these rocks which was nearest to Italy, there was a cave, in which dwelt Scylla, a fearful monster, barking like a dog. In the opposite rock dwelt Charybdis, who thrice every day swallowed down the waters of the sea, and thrice threw them up again"—*Classical Dictionary*. There was a proverbial line, *incidis in Scyllam cupiens vitare Charybdim*, 'in seeking to avoid Charybdis you fall into Scylla,' i.e. escape one danger only to fall into another.

Editors note that Milton has in mind a passage in Silius Italicus (a late Latin poet, of the 'silver age'), where the two monsters are represented as charmed by the pipe of a shepherd. Milton's figure of Sin in *Par. Lost*, II. 650 et seq. reflects the influence of the classical accounts of Scylla.

barking; cf. *Odyssey*, XII. 85, "therein dwelleth Scylla, yelping terribly (δεινὸν λελακυῖα)." Vergil speaks of a rock

surrounded by "barking waves" (*multis circum latrantibus undis*
—*Æneid*, VII. 588).

261. *robbed it of itself*, i.e. made it unconscious.

262. *home-felt*, 'keenly felt'; *home* suggesting 'to the full.'
As we say, 'pay him home,' 'drive it home.'

263. *sober;* in contrast to "madness" (261), as "waking"
to "slumber" (260). *This* (says Comus) is an elevated pleasure
which one enjoys with all the faculties keenly awake to it and
not soothed into unconsciousness.

265. Cf. Ferdinand's meeting with Miranda, *The Tempest*,
I. 2. 425—427:

> "my prime request,
> Which I do last pronounce, is, O you wonder!
> If you be maid or no?"

267, 268. i.e. unless thou art the goddess that dwells here.

268. *Sylvan. Sylvanus*, originally the god of fields and
forests (Lat. *silva*, a wood), was in later times identified with
Pan, the god of nature in general (Gk. πᾶν, all).

blest song; referring to the strains he has just heard.

269. Cf. *Arcades*, 48, 49.

271. *shepherd.* See 164—167. *ill is lost*, i.e. *male perditur.*

273. *boast of skill*, i.e. boastful desire to show her skill.

extreme shift; scan *éxtreme*, an illustration of the rule that
in Shakespeare and Milton words like *obscúre, extréme, compléte*,
throw the accent on to the previous syllable when they are followed immediately by an accented syllable, e.g. a monosyllable
like *shift.* Cf. *Lucrece*, 230, "And éxtreme fear can neither
fight nor fly." So "sérene air" (4), "cómplete steel" (421).

276. *her mossy couch*, i.e. on the "margent green" (232).

277—290. Note the severely classical style. Even in *Samson
Agonistes* (which for Goethe had "more of the antique spirit
than any other production of any other modern poet") we do not
find a piece of στιχομυθία (i.e. dialogue in alternate lines) so long
as the present. The nearest approach is the dialogue between
Manoah and the Messenger, 1552 et seq. There are a few
examples of the same type of dialogue in Shakespeare's earlier
plays; cf. *Richard III.* IV. 4. 343—367, a play written under
the influence of his great predecessor Marlowe. Marlowe was a
Cambridge man, and, though the general character of his works
is essentially romantic, yet he shows the influence of his academic

training by several features, e.g. the use of στιχομυθία and numerous classical allusions. Examples of this kind of dialogue might also be given from the English classical tragedies like *Gorboduc*, in which the model of the late Latin tragic writer Seneca is followed. Seneca himself took the Greek tragedians, especially Euripides, as *his* models.

278. *leavy;* so the original editions, as in *Macbeth*, **v.** 6. 1, "leavy screens." *V* in place of *f* was characteristic of the southern dialects. In the old poem of *The Owl and the Nightingale,* written in Dorsetshire about 1260, we find *vo* for *foe, vairer* for *fairer* etc. (Earle). And the same pronunciation may still be heard any day in Somersetshire; *fallow field* is always (from a labourer) *vallow vield. labyrinth;* cf. "mazes," 181.

279. *near-ushering,* going just ahead. *usher;* see G.

282. She gave rather a different reason in 185, 186.

283. *side;* cf. the use of *latus* in phrases like *tegere latus alicui*=to walk close by the side of.

285. *prevented,* anticipated; see G.

286. *hit,* guess; the metaphor of shooting at a target.
    "But what it is, hard is to say,
        Harder to hit"—*Samson Agonistes,* 1013—14.

287. i.e. 'does the loss of them matter much to you, apart from the inconvenience which it causes you just now?' The question is an indirect way of asking who the two are, what is their connexion with the lady.

290. Cf. *L'Allegro,* 29. Hebe (daughter of Zeus), the cup-bearer of the gods, stands for the personification of blooming youth. Cf. Tennyson, *The Gardener's Daughter:*
    "Her violet eyes, and all her Hebe bloom."

291, 292. A common and natural way of indicating the time of sunset (cf. 188—190) in pastoral verse. Cf. Homer's βουλυτόνδε, 'towards evening, at eventide'; literally 'the time for unyoking oxen' (from βοῦς, an ox + λύειν, to loose). We must remember that Comus appears as a rustic.

what time, at the time when, *quo tempore.* Cf. *Psalm* lvi. 3, "What time I am afraid, I will trust in thee." See *Lyc.* 28.

loose, i.e. loosed from the plough which is left in the "furrow." Pope borrowed the couplet in his *Pastorals* (III.):
    "While labouring oxen, spent with toil and heat,
        In their loose traces from the field retreat."

293. *swinked*, weary; see G.

295. *yon.* Pointing to some part of the scenery in the background. In *Lyc.* 40, Milton conveys by a single epithet ('gadding') the same picture of the vine's straggling growth.

296. *Plucking clusters;* cf. what the Lady said, 186.

297—301. Milton says something complimentary about all who were concerned in the production of *Comus*; cf. 31, note.

297. *port*, bearing; frequent in Shakespeare—"Assume the port of Mars," *Henry V.* prologue 6.

299. *creatures of the element.* According to the common medieval belief, there were four kinds of "demons" or spirits, who respectively inhabited and ruled over the four elements of fire, air, water and earth. Cf. *Il Penseroso*, 93, 94:

> "those demons that are found
>
> In fire, air, flood, or under ground."

They were called Salamanders (spirits of fire), Sylphs (of air), Nymphs (of water), Gnomes (of under ground). Ariel in *The Tempest* is primarily a spirit of air, but is also at home in and has power over the other three elements.

element, air and sky. Cf. "the complexion of the element," i.e. appearance of the sky, *Julius Cæsar*, I. 3. 128.

301. *plighted*, folded; suggesting masses of clouds. Cf. Collins's *Ode to Liberty*, 103, "yon braided clouds." *plighted;* see G. *awe-strook.* Masson notes that Milton usually writes *strook* rather than *struck* both as preterite and past part.

303, 304. The sense has been well explained as "that it would give Comus extreme happiness to accompany the Lady on her quest, with the implication that the quest of such beings [as he has just described] must be a noble one." *Heaven* carries on the idea in "more than human" (297), "creatures of the element" (299); and the whole is a compliment to the Lady.

Some explain : 'to help you find them in this dark wood would be *a task as hard as* the road to Heaven.' But obviously Comus would not discourage the Lady from accompanying him : the hint of difficulty comes from her (307—310), not him (311—321): *his* idea is to encourage and flatter her.

310. *well-practised*, familiar with the wood (180).

311. *each...every;* see 19, note. *alley*, walk, path ; see G.

312. *Dingle.* "A hollow between hills: dale"—*Johnson.*

313. *bosky bourn*, a stream with shrubs and trees on the banks. See each word in the Glossary.

315. *stray*, who have gone astray. *attendance*, attendants; abstract for concrete.

315, 316. *lodged*, i.e. in some cottage (cf. 320, 339, 346). *shroud*, are sheltering, i.e. in the open air, under some tree or bank.

317, 318. i.e. the lark which has her roosting-place ("ground-nest," as he calls it in *Par. Regained*, II. 280) among grass or stubble such as *thatched* roofs are made of. For a similar vague use of *thatch'd* cf. *The Tempest*, IV. 63, where the sense seems to be 'thick-covered as with a thatch.'

319, 320. *low but loyal*, humble but reliable.

322—326. The sentiment reminds us of the Republican Milton of the Commonwealth days.

322. The derivation—*courtesy* from *court*, 325—is correct. Cf. Greene's *Friar Bacon and Friar Bungay*, III. 67, "His courtesy gentle, smelling of the court"; and George Herbert, *The Church-Porch*, "Courtesie grows in court." See *As You Like It*, III. I. 41, 42.

324. *tapestry*, hung with tapestry.

327. *warranted;* in the general sense 'safe, secure.'

329. *Eye me*, keep your watch over me. *square*, adjust.

331. Cf. Dryden, *Æneid*, III. 767, "The stars were mufflec., and the moon was pent." Tennyson in *The Princess* speaks of "A full sea glazed with muffled moonlight," i.e. the light of a moon half hidden by clouds.

332. *wont'st.* The verb *won*, now limited to the participle *wont* or *wonted*, was then still conjugated; cf. "he wont…to sit," i.e. used to, *Nativity Ode*, 10. But as an inflected verb it was commoner in its original sense 'to dwell in,' i.e. be used to a place; cf. *Par. Lost*, VII. 457, "he wons in forest wild." Cf. the cognate Germ. *wohnen*=(1) to dwell, (2) to be wont.

benison ; O. F. *beneison ;* Lat. *benedictio*, blessing.

333. *Stoop.* Cf. the picture in *Il Penseroso*, 71, 72 of the moon "Stooping through a fleecy cloud"; and *Endymion*, IV.:

> "The moon put forth a little diamond peak,
>   Bright signal that she only stooped to tie
>   Her silver sandals."

amber ; exactly descriptive of the fringe of light round

the moon when shining through a cloud. **Cf.** Tennyson's
Margaret, 1.:

> "Like the tender amber round,
> Which the moon about her spreadeth,
> Moving thro' a fleecy night."

"Amber" is the tint of the atmosphere in *The Lotos-Eaters*,
Choric Song v., and of the sunrise in *L'Allegro*, 61 ("Robed in
flames and amber light").

334. *disinherit*, dispossess. *Inherit* in Shakespeare frequently signifies 'to have,' 'possess,' without any notion, as
now, of heirship.

Chaos. Cf. the description of the dark realm of Chaos and
his consort "ancient *Night*" in *Par. Lost*, II. 959 et seq.

336—341. i.e. if your influence (the moon's) be quite eclipsed,
then do thou, Oh gentle taper, from some quarter, visit us, and
thou shalt be, etc.

336. *influence*, power; see G.

340. A beautiful instance of the sound echoing the sense.
The alliteration (*l. l.*) is clearly meant to suggest the line of light.
Cf. Matthew Arnold's *The Scholar-Gipsy*, "The line of festal
light in Christ-Church Hall." For *l. l.* suggesting length see
Par. Lost, VII. 480.

341, 342. A somewhat fanciful way of saying that they will
direct their course by the light of the taper as a mariner directs his
course by means of the constellations. *star of Arcady* = any star in
the constellation of the Great Bear (*Ursa major*). *Cynosure* =
the constellation of the Lesser Bear (*Ursa minor*), especially the
star at the end of the tail, known as the Pole-star; the name
Cynosure being due to the constellation's supposed resemblance to
the shape of a dog's tail (κυνὸς οὐρά). The story ran that the
Arcadian nymph Callisto, after being turned into a she-bear by
Juno, was changed into a star, the Great Bear, by Jupiter. She
was the daughter of Lycaon, king of *Arcadia:* whence Milton's
"star of *Arcady.*" Arcas, the son of Callisto, was changed into
the Lesser Bear. Greek sailors steered by the Great Bear;
the Phœnicians (or *Tyrians*) by the Lesser—hence "*Tyrian*
Cynosure." For the same reason the Lesser Bear was also
called Φοινίκη (the *Phœnician* star). See *Class. Dictionary*.

As *Cynosura* meant literally the star to which sailors looked,
Cynosure came to signify metaphorically (1) 'a guiding star,'

(2) 'an object on which attention is specially fixed.' For (1) cf. Sylvester's *Du Bartas*, Grosart's ed., vol. I. p. 88 :

> "To the bright Lamp which serves for *Cynosure*
> To all that sail upon the sea obscure."

This sense, now obsolete, is required by the present verse in *Comus*. For (2) cf. *L'Allegro*, 80, "The Cynosure of neighbouring eyes."

344. *wattled cotes*, i.e. sheepfolds made with small hurdles. Matthew Arnold borrowed the phrase in *The Scholar-Gipsy*: "Go, shepherd, and untie the wattled cotes"; and Tennyson varied it in the *Ode to Memory*, IV.:

> "Pour round mine ears the livelong bleat
> Of the thick-fleeced sheep from wattled folds."

Wattle='hurdle' is the same word as *wallet*='a bag.'

345. *pastoral reed*, the traditional shepherd's pipe. See 823.

The *oaten* pipe has been accepted by English writers as distinctly symbolical of pastoral music, without, as Mr Jerram points out in his note on *Lyc.* 33, any direct authority in the classics. In Theocritus we have the κάλαμος (i.e. reed) and Pan's pipe, σῦριγξ ; in Latin poets *calamus, tibia* and *cicuta* (the stem of hemlock). Probably the notion of the "oaten straw" is to be traced to Vergil's *tenui avena*, in the first *Eclogue*, 2. Cf. the *Glosse* to the *Shepheards Calender*, October, "Oaten reedes, Avena." But *avena* could be applied to any stalk.

stops; the small holes in wind instruments like the flute. Cf. *Hamlet*, III. 2. 365–376: "Will you play upon this *pipe?*... 'Tis as easy as lying: govern these *ventages* with your finger and thumb...these are the *stops.*" Collins, who imitated Milton very often, began his *Ode to Evening* with the words "If aught of oaten stop, or pastoral song..."

346. *the lodge*, i.e. of the keeper of the wood.

349. *innumerous*, innumerable; L. *innumerus*. Cf. *Par. Lost*, VII. 455, "innumerous living creatures." We find much the same shifting use of adjectival and participial terminations in Shakespeare ; e.g. *unvalued*= invaluable, *Richard III.* I. 4. 27 ; *unavoided*=unavoidable, *Richard II.* II. 1. 268 ; *unexpressive*=inexpressible, *As You Like It*, III. 2. 10.

356. *amazement;* a rather stronger word then = utter bewilderment.

358. i.e. "the hunger of savage beasts, or the lust of men as savage as they"—*Newton.*

359. *over-exquisite,* too careful; like Lat. *exquisitus,* subtle.

360. *cast,* i.e. conjecture the nature of; perhaps from the metaphor of casting a nativity. For the sentiment cf. Landor:

> "Oh seek not destined evils to divine,
>
> Found out at last too soon"—*Gebir,* VI.

361. *grant they be so,* grant that they are real evils, not "false alarms" (364).

363. Alluding to the proverb "Do not meet your trouble half-way." Cf. *Much Ado About Nothing,* I. I. 96—98: "Good Signior Leonato, you are come to meet your trouble; the fashion of the world is to avoid cost, and you encounter it."

365. *self-delusion.* Scan the *ion* as *i-ön.* Cf. 413, 457. In Shakespeare and in Milton's early poems the termination *-ion,* especially with words ending in *ction,* such as 'perfec*tion,*' 'affec*tion,*' 'distrac*tion,*' is often treated as two syllables, especially at the end of a line. In Middle English poetry the termination *-ion* was always treated as two syllables.

366. *so to seek,* so ignorant what to do, so much at a loss. The phrase implies incapacity, or want of knowledge; cf. "they do daylie practise and exercise themselves in the discipline of warre...lest they should be to seek in the feate of armes"—*Utopia,* p. 131, Pitt Press ed. We still say that a quality is 'sadly to seek' in a man, meaning that he lacks it.

367. *unprincipled,* unversed in the principles of. Cf. *principled* in *Samson Agonistes,* 760, =instructed.

368. *bosoms,* i.e. the peace which goodness has in its bosom. Cf. *bosom* used as a verb='enclose in the heart,' 'carefully guard,' in *Henry VIII.* I. I. 112, "bosom up my counsel."

369. *single,* mere. *light and noise.* The Elder Brother had spoken of the darkness, the Younger of the silence.

370. i.e. *she* not being; the absolute case with the pronoun omitted, though easily supplied from the context.

371. The alliteration (*c. c. c.*) emphasises the idea of composure. *constant,* firm, not easily disturbed.

373—375. A reminiscence of *The Faerie Queene,* I. I. 12, "Vertue gives her selfe light through darknesse for to wade."

375. *flat.* Cf. "the level brine" in *Lyc.* 98.

Wisdom's self='Wisdom herself' would sound awkward in

modern E.; but the usage was once common; cf. *Coriolanus*, II. 2. 98, "Tarquin's self he met."

Mr Mark Pattison notes that lines 375—380 possess a personal interest. They are as it were a fragment of the poet's autobiography, descriptive of the years he spent at Horton, 1632—1637. Throughout the poems we catch glimpses of Milton the man.

376. *seeks to*, repairs to; cf. 1 *Kings* x. 24, "And all the earth sought to Solomon, to hear his wisdom"; and *Deuteronomy* xii. 5, "unto his habitation shall ye seek."

378. *plumes ;* some would change to the more usual word *prune.* "A hawk *prunes* when she picks out damaged feathers, and arranges her plumage with her bill "—*Dyce.*

380. *all to-ruffled*, very much ruffled. Milton's editions have *all to ruff'd*, i.e. three distinct words, and there is much difference of opinion as to the right reading.

The difficulty lies with *to*. It is the prefix *to-* =asunder (Germ. *zer*, Lat. *dis*) which is compounded with many Middle E. verbs, giving the sense 'to pieces.' Cf. *to-breken*, to break in pieces (literally 'asunder') ; *to-fallen*, to fall to pieces ; *to-hewen*, to hew to pieces etc. Verbs thus compounded were often strengthened by the adverb *all* preceding them.

Peculiar idioms come gradually to be misunderstood, and variations in their use arise : so with this.

(1) Sometimes *all* and *to* and the verb are separated ; cf. the original reading here and *Judges* ix. 53 : "And a certain woman cast a piece of a millstone upon Abimelech's head, and all to brake his scull."

(2) Sometimes *all*, *to* and the verb are joined ; cf. Bunyan's *Pilgrim's Progress*, II. 48, "she all-to-befooled me."

(3) Sometimes *to* is detached from the verb but united by force of accent with the *all ;* cf. *Latimer's Sermons*, 1538, "We be fallen into the dirt, and be all-to dirtied, even up to the ears."

According therefore to popular usage Milton might equally well write *all to ruffled* (as he did) ; *all-to-ruffled; all-to ruffled ;* and *all to-ruffled.* The last is the most correct (since the *to-* should really go with the verb), and seems the best change if we change at all instead of leaving the idiom as in *Judges* ix. 53. Some editors prefer *all-to ruffled*, but it is not what Milton wrote,

and it gives surely a less pleasing rhythm ; for reading the line
alike quickly or slowly we cannot help treating it as a pure
iambic verse in which *to* goes closely with the following, not the
preceding, word.

To print *all too ruffled* loses the idiom entirely. See the
New English Dictionary under *all-to*.

381. *light within his breast;* the "inward light" of which
he speaks in *Samson Agonistes,* 162, and *Par. Lost,* III. 51—55.

382. *the centre,* i.e. of the earth. Hamlet would find
  "Where truth is hid, though it were hid indeed
    Within the centre"—II. 2. 157—159.

385. See 256 ("prisoned"); cf. *Samson Agonistes,* 155, 156:
  "Thou art become (O worst imprisonment!)
    The dungeon of thyself."

385—392. Cf. *Il Penseroso,* 167—174, which paints the ideal
close of the studious life, and *Richard II.* III. 3. 147—150:
        "I'll give my jewels for a set of beads,
          My gorgeous palace for a hermitage,
          My gay apparel for an alms-man's gown,
          My figured goblets for a dish of wood."

386. *affects,* likes, has affection for.

388. Milton's anticipation of Gray's more felicitous "Far
from the madding crowd's ignoble strife" (*Elegy,* 73).

389. *a senate-house.* Milton was thinking of the Roman
Senate-house, the *Curia.* Twenty years later Cromwell showed,
April 20th, 1653, that the great English Council-chamber was
not inviolable.

390. *hermit;* literally one who dwells in a "desert" (387),
as did the hermits of old; Gk. ἐρημίτης, from ἐρημία, a desert.

391. *beads,* i.e. of the rosary. Every detail in the description—*cell, weeds, grey hairs* etc.—reproduces the conventional
picture of hermit-life. If Milton had written *Comus* after his return
from Italy, we might have thought that in these lines he was
simply repainting in words some picture seen in an Italian palace.

Bead originally meant *prayer;* afterwards the perforated
balls used by Roman Catholics in counting their prayers were
called *beads.* The verb *bid*=to pray (distinct from *bid*=to command) is extant in '*bidding*-prayer.' Cf. Germ. *gebet,* prayer.

393—396. Alluding to the golden apples which Ge (the
Earth) gave to Hera (Juno) on her marriage with Zeus. They

grew in "gardens fair" (981) on an island in the far West, and were watched by the nymphs called the Hesperides (982), who were assisted in their watch by the "dragon" (395) Ladon. To slay the dragon and obtain the apples was one of the labours of Hercules. See *Par. Lost*, III. 568 ("those Hesperian Gardens famed of old") and IV. 250. There is a hitherto unpublished poem on the *Hesperides* by Tennyson in his *Life*.

394, 395. i.e. would need dragons to watch over her with eyes that cannot be enchanted, in order to save etc.

398. *unsunned*, i.e. secret.

401. *wink on*, be blind to. Cf. *Macbeth*, I. 4. 51, 52:

"Let not light see my black and deep desires:
   The eye wink at the hand,"

i.e. let not the eye perceive what the hand is doing. This seems to suit our text. 'Danger' is not to see its opportunity, and, not seeing, is to let the maiden pass unmolested ; a thing, argues the brother, for which we cannot hope. But the personification of Danger is strained. *Desire* would be simpler.

Opportunity. Cf. *Lucrece*, 876 et seq.:

"O Opportunity! thy guilt is great:
   'Tis thou that executest the traitor's treason."

King John put the same truth differently, IV. 2. 219, 220:

"How oft the sight of means to do ill deeds
   Makes ill deeds done."

404. *recks*. Cf. *Lyc.* 122. The verb is not often impersonal.

407. *unowned*, lonely.

408. *Infer*, argue.

409. *without*, beyond; cf. 2 *Corinthians* x. 13, "things without our measure." Cf. the adverb *without*=outside.

410—412. i.e. where the chances seem equally balanced, there being as much reason for hope as for fear, I incline to hope.

411. *arbitrate the event*, decide the issue (= Lat. *eventus*).

413. *squint*, i.e. which does not look at things in a fair, straightforward manner.

418. As Masson observes, we have here, up to 475, the most continuous exposition that *Comus* contains of its central doctrine. The idea is never absent from Milton's thoughts ; but in no other part of the poem is it treated at such length.

419. *if*, even if.

420—424. Probably Milton was thinking of the description of Parthenia in Phineas Fletcher's *Purple Island*, x. 27—32:

> "A warlike maid,
> Parthenia, all in steel and gilded arms."

(*Parthenia*=the Maiden, from Gk. παρθένος, a virgin.)

421. Scan *cómplete*; see 273, note, and cf. *Hamlet*, I. 4. 51—53:

> "What may this mean,
> That thou, dead corse, again in *cómplete* steel
> Revisit'st thus the glimpses of the moon?"

422. *a quivered nymph;* such as those who attended on Diana (see 441).

423. *trace*, pass, wander, through; cf. *A Midsummer-Night's Dream*, II. I. 25, "to trace the forests wild."

unharboured, i.e. unharbouring='yielding no *shelter*,' the proper sense of *harbour*. Cf. Tennyson's *Geraint and Enid*, "O friend, I seek a harbourage for the night." See G.

424. *Infamous hills*. Cf. "And now he haunts th'infamous woods and downs," Phineas Fletcher, *Piscatorie Eclogues*, I. 14. *Infamous*='of evil name,' a Latinism; cf. Horace's *infames scopulos*, *Odes*, I. 3. 20.

The (Latin) accentuation, *infámous*, occurs in the *Death of a Fair Infant*, 12: "Thereby to wipe away the infámous blot."

426. *bandite;* "so spelt in Milton's editions, and probably rather a new word about Milton's time"—*Masson*. From Ital. *bandito*, literally a man placed under the *ban*, i.e. excommunicated by proclamation of the Church.

mountaineer. An opprobrious term, as always in Shakespeare; cf. "call'd me traitor, mountaineer," *Cymbeline*, IV. 2. 120. People who lived in mountain-districts might naturally be taken as types of savage un-civilization.

428. *very*, utter. In Shakespeare *very* is oftener adjective than adverb, being used, as here, to emphasise the noun.

429. *shagged;* cf. *Lyc.* 54. *with horrid shades*, i.e. *horrentibus umbris*. Poets in whom the classical influence is strong use *horrid* of woods because the Latin *horridus* (=shaggy) is a favourite epithet of woodland scenery.

430. *unblenched*, unfaltering: "if he but blench I know my course," says Hamlet (II. 2. 626). Akin to *blanch*.

431. *Be it not*, provided that it be not.

432. *Some say;* a convenient phrase by which he can mention a popular superstition or theory without committing himself to belief in it. Cf. *Par. Lost*, x. 575, 668, 671.

walks. The regular term; see note on 435.

433. *fire*, i.e. a false flame (*ignis futuus*) such as was supposed to attend malicious spirits like Will-o'-the-Wisp and Jack-o'-the-Lanthorn, who loved to " Mislead the amazed night-wanderer from his way" (*Par. Lost*, ix. 640). See *L'Allegro*, 104.

lake or fen. In Ben Jonson's *Masque of Queens* eleven witches appear,

" From the lakes, and from the fens,

From the rocks, and from the dens";

and the author, who was very learned in all pertaining to witchcraft and the like, explains in a footnote that "these places, in their own nature dire and dismal, are reckoned up as the fittest from whence such persons should come."

434. *Blue* = 'livid, haggard,' was a traditional epithet of witches and hags. Cf. "*blue*-eyed hag" (the witch Sycorax, mother of Caliban), i.e. with dark circles under the eyes, such as come from exhaustion or weeping (*The Tempest*, I. 2. 269). *meagre*, lean, F. *maigre*.

stubborn, because refusing to be exorcised or 'laid.' Cf. *Cymbeline*, iv. 2. 278, " *Ghost unlaid* forbear thee!" It was thought that the only tongue in which a spirit could be addressed with effect was Latin; cf. *Hamlet*, I. 1. 42.

435. *magic chains.* Cf. "each fettered ghost," *Nativity Ode*, 234. *curfew time*, usually eight o'clock; cf. *Il Penseroso*, 74. The "foul fiend" in *Lear*, iii. 4. 121, "begins at curfew, and walks till the first cock"; and the spirits in *The Tempest*, v. 39, 40, "rejoice to hear the solemn curfew." See G.

436. *goblin;* see G. *swart;* cf. *Lyc.* 138. *faery.* Rarely used, as here, of a malignant power; cf. *The Comedy of Errors*, iv. 2. 35, "A fiend, a fairy, pitiless and rough"; where, however, many editors change to *fury*.

of the mine. It was an old superstition that mines were inhabited by spirits (i.e. the 'demons' of earth—see note on 299). Collins refers to it in his *Ode to Fear*, speaking of the eve,

"When goblins haunt, from fire or fen,

Or mine, or flood, the walks of men";

and Keats in *Lamia*: "Empty the haunted air and gnoméd mine," i.e. mine where gnomes (sprites) dwell.

438—440. Shall I appeal to the works of Greek philosophers for testimony to the power of purity?

schools, i.e. of philosophy. For *school*=a sect professing a special doctrine, cf. *Samson Agonistes*, 297, "For of such doctrine never was there school."

441. *Dian*, Diana, the maiden goddess of the chase, type of virginity. Cf. Ben Jonson's pretty lines "Queen and huntress, chaste and fair."

443. *brinded*, striped, streaked; see G.

444. *mountain-pard*, a kind of wild-cat, usually called *cat-o'-mountain*, as in *The Tempest*, IV. I. 262.

445. *bolt of Cupid*, i.e. arrow; cf. the famous passage (one of the most exquisite pieces of flattery in all literature) in *A Midsummer-Night's Dream*, II. I. 155—168), where "Cupid all arm'd" takes his vain aim at the "fair vestal" of the West, i.e. Queen Elizabeth. Cupid was said to have two kinds of darts, one with a golden, the other with a leaden tip; the former to cause, the latter to repel, love.

447—452. Milton points the moral; and we may here note how he has taken two old-world, seemingly outworn legends and has invested them with an entirely new significance. It is Plato's method. Plato will often select some popular expression and apply it in a novel, metaphysical sense; or some popular belief, and read into it a fresh meaning, thereby raising superstition to the higher plane of philosophy.

447. The *Gorgoneion* or head of Medusa, whom Perseus had slain, was fixed upon the ægis or shield of Athene (=Lat. Minerva). Cf. *Iliad*, V. 738—741: "about her shoulders cast she (viz. Athene) the tasselled ægis terrible......and therein is the dreadful monster's Gorgon head, dreadful and grim, portent of ægis-bearing Zeus."

snaky-headed, because Medusa's hair had been changed into serpents by Athene; whence her head became so terrible that all who looked on it were turned to stone. There were three Gorgons, monstrous beings, sisters, of whom Medusa is most mentioned in classical writers.

449. *freezed*. The weak form of the preterite was not uncommon in contemporary writers. The strong verbs

suffer perpetually from the incursions of the weak conjugation.

freezed her foes; note the agreement of sense and sound, the alliteration and sibilants suggesting a petrifying shudder and horror. For the scansion *cóngealed* see again the note on 273.

451. *dashed,* put out of countenance, confounded; cf. *Par. Lost,* II. 114.

452. *blank,* utterly dismayed; this use of the adj. is somewhat colloquial. For *blank* as a verb=to make to turn pale, literally 'white' (F. *blanc*),—in fact, to *blench*—cf. *Samson Agonistes,* 471, "And with confusion blank his worshippers."

453. "The language of mythological allusion now ceases, and the speaker passes, in his own name, into a strain of Platonic philosophy tinged with Christianity"—*Masson.*

454. *sincerely,* entirely. Cf. *sincere*=pure, without alloy (L. *sincerus*) in 1 *Peter* ii. 2, "desire the sincere milk of the word." *so,* i.e. chaste.

455. *liveried,* i.e. in all their celestial array; cf. the description of the six pairs of wings and "feathered mail" of the archangel Raphael in *Par. Lost,* V. 277—285. *liveried;* see G.

lackey, attend. *Lackeying* is Theobald's fine emendation in *Antony and Cleopatra,* I. 4. 46, where the Folios read *lacking*— "Goes to and back, lackeying the varying tide." The word has deteriorated somewhat.

This idea of the Guardian Angel watching over men is a favourite with Milton. See 658 and *Par. Lost,* II. 1033. In his theological treatise *The Christian Doctrine* he devotes a section (IX.) to the ministry on earth of angelic beings.

457. *dream...vision.* Cf. Cowley's *Essays:* "I fell at last into this vision; or if you please to call it but a dream, I shall not take it ill, because the father of poets Homer tells us, even dreams too are from God"; where Dr Lumby's note (Pitt Press ed. p. 197) is:

"In *visions* a higher degree of revelation was supposed to be imparted than in *dreams.* Cf. *Select Discourses of John Smith* p. 184: 'The Jews are wont to make a vision superior to a dream, as representing things more to the life.'" The same distinction is seen in Bacon's *Advancement of Learning,* I. 3. 3.

459—463. This fine conception of self-perfectibility, "till body up to spirit work," is developed in *Par. Lost,* V. 469—503;

see especially 496—499, where Raphael tells Adam that if he
and his descendants live pure, sinless lives then perhaps

> "Your bodies may at last turn all to spirit,
>
> Improved by tract of time, and wing'd ascend
>
> Ethereal, as we."

459. *converse*. In the three passages in Shakespeare where
converse='intercourse' occurs the stress falls, as here, on the
second syllable—*convérse*. Cf. *Othello*, III. 1. 40.

461. *temple of the mind*. Scriptural imagery; cf. *John*
ii. 21, "He spake of the temple of his body."

463—469. Milton passes to the converse of the previous
idea. As the body may by self-discipline become soul, the soul
by the self-indulgence of its possessor may become body.

466. "Thou desirest truth in the inward parts," *Psalm* li. 6.

468. i.e. grows fleshly and brutish. Cf. *Par. Lost*, IX. 166,
167, "This essence to incarnate and imbrute!"

469. *property*, essential character, Lat. *proprius*, own.

470—475. Milton here adapts a well-known passage in
Plato's *Phædo*, 81, which Professor Jowett renders:

" But the soul which has been polluted...and is the companion
and servant of the body always, and is in love with and fascinated
by the body......do you suppose that such a soul will depart pure
and unalloyed?

That is impossible, he replied.

She is engrossed by the corporeal, which the continual
association and constant care of the body have made natural to
her.

Very true.

And this, my friend, may be conceived to be that heavy,
weighty, earthy element of sight by which such a soul is
depressed and dragged down again into the visible world,
because she is afraid of the invisible and of the world below—
prowling about tombs and sepulchres, in the neighbourhood of
which, as they tell us, are seen certain *ghostly apparitions of
souls* which have not departed pure, but are cloyed with sight
and therefore visible." *Dialogues of Plato*, vol. I. p. 429.

It was, no doubt, belief in the continued association
of body and soul after death, and the durability of the
former, that led to the yearly offering of meat and drink, and
even clothes, at tombs—*Thucydides*, III. 58. Many popular

superstitions as to the attachment which the soul feels for its corporeal tenement might be instanced; e.g. the old Bohemian idea that the *anima* of a dead man took the form of a bird and perched upon a tree near to the spot where the body was being burnt. When the latter was consumed the soul flitted away.

470. *gloomy shadows damp*. Plato's phrase is ψυχῶν σκιοειδῆ φαντάσματα. For the word-order cf. 207, note.

471. i.e. περὶ τὰ μνήματά τε καὶ τοὺς τάφους κυλινδουμένη, as Plato says of the soul; see the words italicised in extract above.

473. *it;* properly *they*, "gloomy shadows" being the subject; but *it* is more vivid, drawing the eye of imagination to some particular dim shadow.

474. *sensualty;* so the original editions, to suit the metre.

478. Cf. Biron's description of love in *Love's Labour's Lost*, IV. 3. 342—343:

"Subtle as Sphinx; as sweet and musical
As bright Apollo's lute."

There is a certain humour in transferring the phrase to philosophy. The editors cite Milton's *Tractate of Education* (1644): "I shall detain you now no longer in the demonstration of what we should not do, but straight conduct you to a hill-side, where I will point you out the right path of a virtuous and noble education; laborious indeed at the first ascent, but else so smooth, so green, so full of goodly prospect, and melodious sounds on every side, that the harp of Orpheus was not more charming."

479. *nectared*, sweet as nectar, the drink of the gods.

480. *crude*, i.e. undigested, =Lat. *crudus;* see *Lyc.* 3.

483. *night-foundered*, overtaken by, or plunged in, night; cf. *Par. Lost*, I. 204, "The pilot of some small night-foundered skiff."

486. *Again, again!* i.e. the shout.

487. *draw*, i.e. their swords.

489. Cf. the sentiment of the king in 2 *Henry VI.* III. 2. 233: "Thrice is he armed that hath his quarrel just."

habited, dressed. *like a shepherd;* cf. 84—91.

490. *That hallo.* The Elder Brother called out, 487, and the Attendant Spirit answered. His reply is marked in the stage-direction of Lawes's edition, 1637. In line 490, therefore,

"that" refers to the answer given by Thyrsis before he appears on the stage.

491. i.e. they present their swords.

494. *Thyrsis.* A traditional shepherd name as far back as Theocritus; cf. his first *Idyl*, and Vergil's seventh *Eclogue*. In the *Epitaphium Damonis*, 4, the pastoral Latin elegy in which he laments the death of his friend Diodati under the guise of one shepherd mourning for another, Milton speaks of himself as Thyrsis. Matthew Arnold's Monody (*Thyrsis*) on Clough lent the name new life and associations.

The lines, 494—496, are an intentional compliment to Lawes, and a more delicate compliment than the other (86—88), which was placed in Lawes's own mouth—*Newton.*

495—512. Note the rhyme and Masson's explanation, viz. that having mentioned the word *madrigal* in 495 Milton wished to carry on for a moment the idea of pastoral poetry which *madrigal* (see G.) suggests. The heroic couplet had been much associated with pastoral verse; e.g. in a considerable portion of *The Shepheards Calender*. Ben Jonson in the *Sad Shepherd* gives us the same combination of blank verse, rhymed decasyllabic couplets, and periodic lyrics.

495. *huddling;* because the waters stop in their course to listen, and thus crowd together; some, however, interpret 'hastening, pressing onward,' i.e. so as to listen. Milton refers to the classical stories how the music of the golden lyre of Orpheus enchanted all nature, "delaying (says Horace, *Odes*, I. 12. 9, 10) even the swift-flowing streams."

501. *his next joy*, i.e. the Second Brother.

502. *toy*, trifle; see G.

506. *to*, compared to; from the idea 'in relation to.' Cf. "Hyperion to a satyr," *Hamlet*, I. 2. 140.

the care it brought, the anxiety which I brought on my errand.

507. Strictly the question is unnecessary. Thyrsis knew that the Lady was in the power of Comus; cf. 571—578. But the enquiry leads up to the explanation that follows.

508. *How chance?* The verb-construction 'how does it chance that?' is influenced by the noun-phrase 'by what chance?' Cf. "How chance the roses there do fade so fast?"—*A Midsummer-Night's Dream*, I. 1. 129. See Abbott's *Shakespearian Grammar*, p. 40.

509. *sadly*, seriously; cf. *Romeo and Juliet*, I. I. 207, "But sadly tell me who." See *sad* in the Glossary.

without blame; i.e. without any fault of ours.

511, 512. Observe the rhyme, *true* and *shew*, proving that the pronunciation of the latter has entirely changed. Cf. 994—997, and Sonnet II., where *youth* and *shew'th* rhyme.

513. *fabulous*, mere matter of fable, legend (Lat *fabula*).

515. *the sage poets;* meaning Homer and Vergil; Tasso (familiar to Elizabethans in the fine translation of Fairfax) and Ariosto; and Spenser—especially Spenser, who influenced Milton greatly. Cf. the publisher's preface to the 1645 ed. of Milton's poems: "I shall deserve of the age by bringing into the light as true a birth as the Muses have brought forth since our famous Spenser wrote; whose poems in these...are as rarely imitated as sweetly excelled." Cf. the reference to "our admired Spenser" in the *Animadversions (P. W.* III. 84, 85), where Milton quotes at some length from *The Shepheards Calender*, Maye. Spenser is the "*sage* and serious poet" of the *Areopagitica*, *P. W.* II. 68, where *The Faerie Queene*, II. 7, is in Milton's thoughts. In the preface to his *Fables* (translations from Chaucer and Boccacio) Dryden writes: "Milton was the poetical son of Spenser......Milton has acknowledged to me that Spenser was his original."

taught by the heavenly Muse. Repeated in *Par. Lost*, III. 19:

"I sung of Chaos and eternal Night,
Taught by the Heavenly Muse."

This claim to direct inspiration is common with poets influenced by the classics. Milton is so great, and so justly conscious of his greatness, that coming from him the words have no trace of boastful egotism.

516. *Storied*, narrated. Cf. *Venus and Adonis*, 1013, 1014.

517. Cf. *Par. Lost*, II. 628, "Gorgons, and Hydras, and Chimæras dire." Milton's poetry is full of these verbal echoes; partly because he so often employs traditional epithets, taken straight from the classics. For the Chimæra cf. *Iliad*, VI. 181: πρόσθε λέων, ὄπιθεν δὲ δράκων, μέσση δὲ χίμαιρα, i.e. it was a monster resembling a lion in its fore part, a dragon in its hind part, and a goat in the middle.

enchanted isles. Referring primarily, we can scarcely doubt, to the "Wandring Islands" of *The Faerie Queene*, II. 12. 11 et seq. Spenser followed Tasso's account of the isle of Armida.

518. *rifted*, i.e. rocks with yawning chasms. *Rift*=to split, closely akin to *rive*, occurs in *The Winter's Tale*, V. I. 66.

520. *navel*, centre; an imitation of the similar use of Gk. ὄμφαλος, a navel, and Lat. *umbilicus*. Byron coined a participle *navelled*=set in the midst of; cf. "Nemi navelled in the woody hills," *Childe Harold*, IV. 173.

521. *cypress*; the gloomiest of shade, hence appropriate to the scene of the horrid "rites" (535) of the magician and his "monstrous rout."

522—530. Cf. 46—77.

526. *murmurs*, i.e. incantations spoken over the potion as it was being brewed, such as those of the Witches in *Macbeth*, IV. I. For *murmur*=spell, cf. *Arcades*, 60, "With puissant words, and murmurs made to bless."

529, 530. i.e. destroying the emblem of reason which is stamped in the human countenance. George Herbert says in *The Church-Porch*, "Wine above all things doth God's stamp deface."

529. *reason*; for Milton, the chief faculty of the soul (*Par. Lost*, V. 100—102); the embodiment of those higher qualities of intellect which separate men from the brute creation.

530. *Charactered*, stamped; a continuation of the metaphor in *unmoulding* (i.e. breaking up the pattern) and *mintage* See G., and for the accentuation cf. *The Two Gentlemen of Verona*, II. 7. 3, 4:

> "the table wherein all my thoughts
> Are visibly *charácter'd* and engraved."

531. *croft*. "A little close [i.e. enclosure] adjoining to a house, and used for corn or pasture"—*Johnson*.

532. *That brow this bottom glade*, i.e. that skirt the top of the wood which slopes down to the valley. In some dialects (e.g. the New Forest) *bottom* is still in use for a valley, glade.

533. *monstrous rout*, herd of monsters; an instance of the adjective doing the duty of the first part of a compound noun; cf. *Lyc.* 158. *Monster-rout* would sound awkward. German has a distinct advantage over English in this respect.

534. Perhaps *stabled*= 'which have got inside the sheep-fold (Lat. *stabulum*),' and, as we know from Vergil, *Eclogue* III. 80, *triste lupus stabulis* ('a wolf is no pleasant thing for sheepfolds').

But Milton may only mean 'wolves in their haunts'; cf. *Par. Lost*, XI. 752, where the verb *stable*=to have a lair.

535. *Doing rites;* Lat. *sacra facere*, Gk. ἱερὰ ῥέζειν.

abhorred, detest*able*, horrible; for the termination *ed*=*able* see the note on 349. *Hecate;* see 135, note.

537. *yet*, i.e. though they themselves are "monstrous" and therefore repulsive, and their "rites" horrible, *yet* they have means to attract people.

539. Milton, like Spenser, uses *unweeting*, not *unwitting*. The *ee* represents better the long *i* of A.-S. *witan*, to know.

540. *by then*, by the time that. Cf. *by this*='by this time'; "And I do know, by this, they stay for me," *Julius Cæsar*, I. 3. 125.

542. *knot-grass*. There is a stock joke in the dramatists that short people have eaten knot-grass (*Polygonum aviculare*), whose special property it was to stop growth. Cf. *A Midsummer-Night's Dream*, III. 2. 329 ("*hindering* knot-grass").

546. *pleasing...melancholy*. Not gloomy dejection, but the serious, meditative mood celebrated in *Il Penseroso* (see 175, "these *pleasures*" etc.); what Gray in a letter calls "white Melancholy, or rather *Leucocholy*." Gk. λευκός=white.

547. i.e. to play on my shepherd's pipe. See *Lyc.* 66.

548. *her fill;* now a somewhat vulgar phrase, but not then; cf. Sonnet XIV. 14, "And drink thy fill of pure immortal streams." See *Leviticus* xxv. 19.

ere a close; "i.e. before he had finished the song he had begun on his pipe"—*Masson*. Possibly *close* has its musical sense 'cadence,' i.e. before he reached a cadence in his song. Cf. *Richard II.* II. 1. 12, "music at the close." A musician himself, Milton uses musical terms often, with a musician's accuracy.

549. *wonted;* cf. "night by night" (532).

was up, had begun. The 'Hunt's up' was the title of an old ballad-tune, referred to in *Romeo and Juliet*, III. 5. 34.

551. *Listen* is transitive in *Much Ado About Nothing*, III. 1. 12, "listen our purpose" (=hear our conversation, F. *propos*).

552. *an unusual stop*, i.e. at line 145 ("break off").

553. *respite*, i.e. "from the trouble the noise had been causing them"—*Masson*.

drowsy-flighted; so the *Cambridge MS.*, except that the

words are not hyphened. The original editions (1637, 1645, 1673) all have *drowsie frighted*, which must mean, 'the drowsy steeds of night which had been frighted by the noise of Comus and his crew.' Though this reading has the better authority, it seems in itself much inferior to *drowsy-flighted*. For *drowsy-flighted* gives a more picturesque conception; it is in form an *essentially* Miltonic compound—cf. "flowery-kirtled" (254), "rushy-fringed" (890); and it harmonises with the passage in 2 *Henry VI.* IV. I. 3—6, which Milton must have had in his mind's eye:

"And now loud-howling wolves arouse the jades
  That drag the tragic melancholy night;
  Who with their *drowsy, slow and flagging wings*
  Clip dead men's graves."

We have, surely, in the third line of this quotation the germ of *drowsy-flighted*, and it appears most improbable that Milton should have changed the line so manifestly for the worse. Further, *drowsy frighted* is an awkward combination of opposite ideas. I suppose then that *frighted* was simply an error in the 1637 edition which escaped Milton's notice and, not being corrected by him, was of course reproduced by the printer in the later editions. Newton first adopted *flighted* from the *Cambridge MS.* and Masson accepts it. The attempt to make *frighted = freighted* (with the sense 'the steeds of night heavy with sleep') is impossible.

554. *litter*, chariot. *close-curtained Sleep*. We cannot help remembering Macbeth's "curtain'd sleep," II. I. 51; and Juliet's "Spread thy close curtain, night," *Romeo*, III. 2. 5.

555—562. Referring of course to the Lady's Song (230—243), in the same complimentary manner as before (244). Gray (*Progress of Poesy*, I. 2) addresses the power of music:

"Oh! Sovereign of the willing soul,
  Parent of sweet and solemn-breathing airs."

556. *stream of perfume*. The edition of 1673 spoils the metaphor by substituting *stream*. Todd quotes a beautiful parallel from Bacon's *Essays* (XLVI.): "Because the breath of flowers is farre sweeter in the aire, where it comes and goes like the warbling of music." Cf. Tennyson, *The Lotos-Eaters*:

"they find a music centred in a doleful song
  Steaming up."

Note in 555—557 the effect of the alliteration (*s...s* and *st*).

557, 558. So when the nightingale sang "Silence was pleased" (*Par. Lost*, IV. 604). *that*, so that. *took*, charmed; see G.

559, 560. i.e. cease to exist, if she could always be displaced or banished in the same way. *still*, ever, always.

560. *all ear;* now a rather colloquial phrase, but not then; cf. *The Tempest*, IV. 59, "No tongue! all eyes! be silent!"

562. *the ribs of Death;* a conventional description. Warburton thought that it might have been suggested by some allegorical representation of Death as a "bare-ribbed" skeleton in a popular *Book of Emblems*. "Bare-ribbed" is the epithet applied to Death in *King John*, V. 2. 177. Contrast the shadowy, more awe-inspiring conception of Death in *Par. Lost*, II. 666—673.

565. *Amazed;* see 356, note.

568. *lawns*, glades, open spaces in the forest; see G.

571. *in sly disguise*, i.e. as a "villager," 166; cf. 576.

575. We are to suppose that he was present, though invisible, at part of the interview between the Lady and Comus. *such two*, i.e. as she described. Cf. "two such I saw," 291.

584. *You gave me.* Referring to 418—458.

585. *period*, sentence.

586. *for me*, as far as I am concerned.

591. i.e. that which mischief intended to be most harmful.

592. *happy trial*, trial of happiness; or the adjective might have what is called a proleptic (or anticipatory) force—'the trial which proves virtue happy.'

593—597. Slowly separating from the good the evil element preys upon itself, just as the figure of Sin in *Par. Lost*, II, 798—800 is gnawed by the whelps of her own womb.

594. *when*, till.

595. *settled;* like liquid; the metaphor in "scum."

597. *if this fail;* if what I have said prove false.

598. Cf. *Par. Regained*, IV. 455, "the pillared frame of heaven," where Mr Jerram's note is: "The (supposed) solid dome of the sky requires pillars for its support." He refers to *Job* xxvi. 11, "the pillars of heaven tremble...at his reproof."

603. *legions.* Scan as a trisyllable. *griesly;* see G.

604. *Acheron.* Strictly one of the four rivers of the lower world round which the shades of the dead hover, as in *Par. Lost*, II. 578:

> "Abhorred Styx, the flood of deadly hate;
> Sad Acheron, of sorrow, black and deep":

then put for the lower world itself; cf. the use of *Stygian*, 132. From ἄχος, pain, sorrow + ῥεεῖν, to flow.

605. *Harpies;* the 'robbers' or 'spoilers,' from Gk. ἁρπάζειν, to seize. They were hideous, winged female monsters with hooked claws, who swooped upon Æneas and his followers as they were feasting in one of the Ionian islands and carried off their food (*Æneid*, III. 225—228). One of the most vivid descriptions of the Harpies in English poetry is in William Morris's *Jason*, V. 219 et seq.

Hydra; literally 'a water serpent' (Gk. ὕδωρ, water); specially used of the *Lernean Hydra*, a nine-headed serpent, the slaying of which was one of the 'labours' of Hercules. When he cut off one head two fresh heads sprang in its stead, till at last he discovered how to deal with the monster.

606. *Twixt Africa and Ind,* i.e. from one end of the world to the other—west to east. *Ind* or *Inde* is a common poetic form of India; cf. *Par. Lost*, II. 2.

608. In Ben Jonson's Masque *Pleasure Reconciled to Virtue*, Comus has "his head crown'd with roses and other flowers, his hair curled." In Elizabethan times curling the hair was a mark of effeminacy and affectation; see *King Lear*, III. 4. 88.

609. *purchase*, prize, booty; see G.

610. *yet*, nevertheless, i.e. though he has just said "alas!" It is vain courage, but he cannot help admiring it.

bold emprise; a frequent Spenserian phrase, with an Italian ring; cf. the first line of Ariosto's *Orlando Furioso*: "Le cortesie, l' audaci imprese, io canto." Also in *Par. Lost*, XI. 642.

611. *stead*, service; cf. the verb in *The Merchant of Venice*, I. 3. 7, "May you stead me?" i.e. Can you help me? To do a thing in the *stead*, i.e. place, of a man is to help him.

612. *other*, i.e. mightier. For the repetition cf. *Lyc*. 174.

614, 615. There are resemblances to *The Tempest;* cf. I. 2. 469—473 (Prospero's first meeting with Ferdinand), IV. 259.

bare, mere. *wand;* the usual symbol of magical power; cf. Prospero's "staff" (V. 54). *unthread*, take out of their sockets, dislocate. *crumble*, cause to shrivel up.

617. *As to make*, i.e. as to be able to make.

relation, report; cf. the verb 'to *relate*.'

618. *surprisal;* an echo of 590.

619—628. Probably a reference to Milton's school-friend Diodati, whose premature death in 1638 inspired the *Epitaphium Damonis*. Lines 150—154 of that poem mention Diodati's knowledge of botany and habit of imparting it to Milton.

620. *to see to.* An obsolete expression = to behold; cf. *Ezekiel* xxiii. 15: "Girded with girdles upon their loins, exceeding in dyed attire upon their heads, all of them princes to look to," and *Joshua* xxii. 10, "a great altar to see to."

skilled, i.e. versed in the lore of. *Skill* was a word of wider scope then. Among the synonyms of it given and illustrated by quotation in Schmidt's *Shakespeare Lexicon* are 'discernment,' 'sagacity,' 'mental power,' 'knowledge of any art.'

621. *virtuous*, possessed of medicinal properties.

626. *scrip*, bag. "Orig. sense 'scrap,' because made of a scrap of stuff"—*Skeat.* Cf. *Luke* xxii. 35.

627. *simples.* A *simple* was a single (i.e. *simple*) ingredient in a compound, especially in a compounded medicine. Its association with medicine led to the common meaning 'medicinal herb'; once in current use, as it occurs so often in Shakespeare—"*culling* of simples," *Romeo and Juliet*, v. 1. 40. Cf. 630.

630—633. In point of style this passage, with its accumulation of *buts*, seems the most awkward in *Comus.*

634. *like*, i.e. correspondingly: 'as unknown, so unesteemed.'

635. *clouted*, patched, mended; see G.

636, 637. *that*, the famous; cf. 2. *Moly;* the mysterious plant which Hermes (Lat. Mercury) gave Odysseus as a safeguard against the charms of Circe (*Odyssey*, x. 281—306). In poetry it is the flower of ideal lands. Tennyson's Lotos-Eaters lie "Propt on beds of amaranth and moly"; and Shelley associates the same plants in *Prometheus Unbound*, II. 4:

"folded Elysian flowers,
Nepenthe, Moly, Amaranth, fadeless blooms."

637. *wise.* Homer's constant epithet for Odysseus (= Ulysses) is πολύμητις = of many counsels, i.e. ever ready with some wise scheme. This conception of him as the man of wonderful knowledge and thought and experience is brought out most strikingly in Tennyson's *Ulysses.*

638. *Hæmony.* The name is Milton's invention and commonly explained as a reference to *Hæmonia*, an old name of Thessaly, the land of magic in classical writers (e.g. Horace, *Odes*, I. 27. 21, 22). So we may call it 'the Thessalian plant.'

639. *sovran*, most efficacious; see G.

640. *mildew blast*, i.e. the hurtful power of mildew sent by evil spirits. Cf. *King Lear*, III, 4. 120, 123, "This is the foul fiend...he mildews the white wheat."

641. *Furies*, evil fairies. Scan *appariti-ón.*

642. i.e. I put it away in my purse, but never thought much about it. See *Lyc.* 116.

644. *it*, i.e. what the shepherd had said about the plant.

644—647. Warton points out that it was a recognised expedient in medieval tales for a warrior of the type of the Red Crosse Knight to carry a charm, often a herb, as a protective against evil influences.

650, 651. Probably an echo of *Odyssey*, X. 294, 295, where Hermes says to Odysseus, "when it shall be that Circe smites thee with her long wand, then draw thou thy sharp sword from thy thigh, and spring on her, as one eager to slay her."

651, 652. So in *The Faerie Queene*, II. 12. 57, when the sorceress Acrasia offered to Guyon the enchanted cup which she was wont to present to strangers, he flung it down, "And with the liquor stained all the land."

653. *seize his wand;* which the brothers fail to do.

curst crew. Cf. *Par. Lost*, VI. 806. In his epics Milton repeatedly applies *crew* to Satan and the rebellious angels.

655. *Vulcan*, the Roman god of fire, and master of the arts, such as working in metals, which need the aid of fire. Hence his "sons" might be expected to "vomit smoke," as did the giant Cacus (one of the "sons"), *Æneid*, VIII. 252, 253.

The Scene changes. Probably a screen, called a *traverse* or *travers*, was put forward while the alteration of the scene was being made. Cf. Ben Jonson's *Entertainment at Theobalds*, 1607, "The King and Queen, being entered into the gallery, after dinner there was seen nothing but a *traverse* of white across the room: which suddenly drawn, was discovered a gloomy obscure place." See Nares's *Glossary.*

soft music. Wanting in the *Cambridge MS.* Doubtless the addition of music was due to Lawes. The idea of tempting by means of a banquet (cf. *The Tempest*, III. 3) meets us in medieval romances of virtue assailed by evil powers. I believe that it is the basis of the scene of temptation in *Par. Regained*, II. 337.

enchanted chair; because "smeared with gums," 917.

puts by, refuses. So Cæsar (I. 2. 230) rejected the crown : "Ay, marry...he put it by thrice." *goes about,* tries.

659—813. Dramatically the most effective part of *Comus*.

660. i.e. your sinews (Lat. *nervi*) will all be turned to alabaster, and you will become a statue, or rooted to the spot, as was Daphne.

For *nerve* in its Latin sense cf. the Sonnet to Vane, where he calls money the "nerves" of war, i.e. sinews, as we say.

are; a vivid present to suggest immediate effect.

alabaster; a sulphate of lime; the pure white variety was much used in images and monuments: hence "statue" in 661. Cf. *The Merchant of Venice*, I. 1. 83, 84:

"Why should a man, whose blood is warm within,

Sit like his grandsire cut in alabaster?"

and "smooth as monumental alabaster" in *Othello*, V. 2. 5.

661. *Daphne.* The story of Daphne the nymph who fled from Apollo and was changed into a laurel-tree at her own petition is told by Ovid, *Metamorphoses*, I. 660 et seq.

664. *corporal rind,* bodily covering.

665. *while,* so long as (and only so long).

668. A reminiscence, perhaps, of *Isaiah* xxxv. 10, "they shall obtain joy and gladness, and sorrow and sighing shall flee away." Comus's temptation of the Lady (especially his arguments later on, 710—736) resembles a scene in the religious play *Adamo* (1613), by the Italian poet Andreini, which deals with the Fall of Man and is thought to have furnished some slight suggestions for *Paradise Lost.* Andreini makes the World personified, with its vanities, tempt Eve, and reading through the scene (V. 5) in the translation by Hayley one is certainly reminded of this scene in *Comus.*

672. *julep.* Properly rose-water; then any bright drink, as here; finally often used to signify a syrup medicine. Persian *gul,* a rose + *áb,* water.

674. *balm;* implying that which soothes.

675, 676. See *Odyssey*, IV. 219—229, where Menelaus and

Helen entertain Telemachus at Sparta; and "Helen, daughter
of Zeus, presently cast a drug into the wine whereof they drank,
a drug to lull all pain and anger, and bring forgetfulness of every
sorrow. Whoso should drink a draught thereof, when it is
mingled in the bowl, on that day he would let no tear fall
down his cheeks, not though his father and mother died.........
Medicines of such virtue (φάρμακα μητιόεντα) had the daughter
of Zeus, which Polydamna, the wife of Thon, had given her, a
woman of Egypt" (Butcher and Lang).

Properly Nepenthes, or Nepenthe, (Gk. νηπενθής, without
pain) meant the drug itself (perhaps opium)—or herb whence it
was extracted—which had this power of lulling sorrow for the
day on which it was drunk : hence any deliciously soothing
liquor. See *The Faerie Queene*, IV. 3. 43.

679. Cf. *Samson Agonistes*, 784, and Shakespeare's first
Sonnet, "Thyself thy foe, to thy sweet self too cruel." In the
translation of More's *Utopia* we read, "When nature biddeth
the (i.e. *thee*) to be good and gentle to other, she commaundeth
the not to be cruell and ungentle to the selfe," p. 107, Pitt Press
ed. Probably the idea was suggested by *Proverbs* xi. 17, "The
merciful man doeth good to his own soul : but he that is cruel
troubleth his own flesh."

680. *Nature lent.* Cf. Shakespeare's fourth Sonnet, 3 :
"Nature's bequest gives nothing, but doth lend," i.e. nature
never gives anything to man for his absolute possession, but
always regards him as holding her gifts on "trust."

685. *unexempt condition,* terms from which no one can be
exempt. Observe how the metaphor of trusteeship runs through
680—685 ; cf. "covenants," "trust," "terms," etc.

686. *mortal frailty,* weak human nature.

688. *That.* The antecedent must be "you" in 682.

693, 694. Cf. 319—321.

695. *aspects,* objects, appearances. Scan *aspécts* and see G.

696. *brewed enchantments,* i.e. the draught in his crystal
cup "with many murmurs mixed" (526). Cf. *Samson Agonistes*,
934, "Thy fair enchanted cup, and warbling charms."

698. *vizored,* masked, disguised. *forgery,* deceit.

700. *lickerish,* dainty; see G.

702, 703. Cf. Euripides, *Medea*, 618, κακοῦ γὰρ ἀνδρὸς δῶρ'
ὄνησιν οὐκ ἔχει ('for the gifts of a bad man bring no advantage');

in the same way 'an enemy's gifts do not profit'—*ἐχθρῶν ἄδωρα δῶρα κοὐκ ὀνήσιμα*, Sophocles, *Ajax*, 665.

706—709. i.e. foolish are those who adopt the doctrines of Stoicism or Cynicism and practise rigid, morose abstinence.

707. *budge;* the name of a fur, perhaps goat-skin; see G. Budge-row in the City was so called because most of the London furriers lived in it; the Skinners' Company's Hall is still there. This fur seems to have been specially employed in the ornamentation of academic dress. Todd quotes a regulation of the University of Cambridge issued in 1414 with reference to the dress of graduates, and budge is one of the furs mentioned as proper for hoods. In a tract against the Presbyterian elders at Belfast Milton refers to their wearing "budge-gowns" (*Observations on the Articles of Peace*). It looks then as if Milton, perhaps with a recollection of budge-trimmed hoods seen at Cambridge, used 'budge' to suggest a learned professor, very much as we use 'ermine' in special association with the judges. I think that we must paraphrase in some such way as 'those teachers whose furred gowns mark them as professors in the school of Stoicism.' There was an adjective *budge*=stiff, formal, solemn-looking; but its use cannot be traced as far as 1634. Moreover, "Stoic *fur*" shows that Milton meant the noun *budge* (=fur), not this adjective. See *New English Dict.*

708. *the Cynic tub.* Referring to Diogenes (B.C. 412—323) the Cynic philosopher, famous for his life of extreme austerity and moroseness at Athens. "He wore coarse clothing, lived on the plainest food, slept in porticoes or in the street, and finally, according to the common story, took up his residence in a tub"—*Classical Dict.* The *Cynics* were so called "from their *dog-like* neglect of all forms and usages of society.' Gk. *κύων*, a dog, whence *κυνικός*, dog-like. The founder of the sect was Antisthenes, a pupil of Socrates.

711. *unwithdrawing*, bounteous, holding back nothing.

712. *odours*, i.e. fragrant herbs and flowers.

714. *But all to*, except to. *curious*, dainty, critical. Cf. Shakespeare, Sonnet 38, 13, "If my slight Muse do please these curious days." Lat. *cura*, care.

716. *shops*, workshops; meaning on mulberry trees.

719. *hutched*, enclosed, shut up; see G. *ore*, metal; see 933, *Lyc.* 170.

721. Cf. *Daniel* i. **12**: "Prove thy servants, I beseech thee, ten days; and let them give us pulse to eat, and water to drink." Cf. *Par. Regained*, II. **278**, "Or as a guest with Daniel at his pulse " (= beans, peas). *a pet of*, a foolish craze for.

722. *frieze*, or *frize*; coarse woollen cloth, made chiefly in Wales; originally however, from *Friesland*. For cloths named after the country whence they were first imported, cf. *Cambric* from *Cambray* in Flanders, *calico* from *Calicut*.

724. *yet despised.* Men would be despising the rich gifts of which they foolishly made no use and therefore could form no just opinion. Cf. **634.**

727. "If ye be without chastisement, whereof all are partakers, then are ye bastards, and not sons," *Hebrews* xii. 8.

like bastards, because the illegitimate have not the same rights as regards their parents that legitimate "sons" have; thus they have no claim to a parent's property at death. But *we* (says Comus) should enjoy the full rights of sonship in relation to our parent Nature.

728, 729. This idea, expanded in the next lines, occurs in *Par. Lost*, V. **318—320.**

surcharged; F. *surchargé*, overladen with. *weight*, i.e. of crops, herds etc. *waste*, wasted.

731. *o'er-multitude*, i.e. grow too numerous for their shepherds and keepers to manage.

732. *o'erfraught*, i.e. overfull of fish ; cf. **713.**

the unsought diamonds. Cf. **881**, where Milton speaks of "diamond rocks." These "rocks" might well be said to "stud" and "emblaze" (i.e. make brilliant) the surface ("forehead") of the sea. The argument seems to be that men should quarry them and take away their diamonds, not leave them there "unsought." Todd argued that the lines were designedly fanciful, and were meant to harmonise "with the character of the 'wily' speaker" (Comus) and "to expose that ostentatious sophistry by which a bad cause is generally supported."

733. Cf. **21—23.**

734. *they below*, i.e. the inhabitants and creatures of the deep, such as mermen, fishes. Some say 'men on earth,' οἱ κάτω.

735. *inured;* see G.

737, 738. Note the contemptuous effect of the alliteration, especially of *c, c.;* so again in **749, 750.** *cozened;* see G.

737—755. The whole passage from "List, lady," 737, down to 755, though extant in the *Cambridge MS.*, is wanting in the Bridgewater copy. This shows that the lines were not spoken at the actual performance. The omission was certainly a great advantage from the point of view of good taste.

738. Cf. Fairfax, translation of Tasso, XIV. 63, "Virtue itself is but an idle name." The line occurs in Tasso's famous description of the isle of Armida; Milton probably had the passage in mind both here and in *Par. Lost*, IV. 272, 273.

739—742. Many parallels, as regards both the sentiment and the language, might be quoted from Elizabethan poets, e.g. Shakespeare's Sonnets, 1—17 (especially 4 and 6 where the metaphor resembles Milton's, viz. money lent at interest); Ben Jonson's *Cynthia's Revels*, I. I (the latter part of Echo's speech "His name revives"); and Drayton's *Legend of Matilda*.

741. *mutual*, shared with others.

743, 744. Cf. *A Midsummer-Night's Dream*, I. I. 76—78.

745. *Nature's brag*, i.e. that of which nature boasts justly.

748. Much the same jingle as "Home-keeping youth have ever homely wits," *The Two Gentlemen of Verona*, I. I. 2.

749, 750. i.e. those who have coarse complexions may be content to ply—that is all very well for *them*, not for you.

complexions. Scan as four syllables. *sorry*, poor, unattractive. *grain;* probably 'hue,' not 'texture' (already implied in "coarse"). See G.

751. *sampler*, a piece of wool-work in which patterns (i.e. *samples*) were designed, especially the alphabet. Lat. *exemplar*, a copy.

to tease, to comb out. In the art of cloth-manufacture *teasing* is the process by which the surface of the cloth is smoothed and roughnesses taken away.

752. *vermeil-tinctured*, red; as if dipped in *vermilion* (from Lat. *vermiculus*, a little worm, used of the cochineal insect).

"Vermeil" as applied to the face represents what has been called "poetic diction," i.e. it is the sort of picturesque description that one poet hands on to another. Cf. Gray, *Ode on Vicissitude*:

> "With vermeil-cheek and whisper soft
> She woos the tardy spring."

and Keats, *Endymion*, IV.:

"O Sorrow,
Why dost borrow
The natural hue of health from vermeil lips?"

753. *Love-darting eyes.* Cf. Sylvester's translation (in exceedingly Spenserian verse) of the French poet Du Bartas: "Whoso beholds her sweet, love-darting eyes" (Grosart's ed. I. 205). This translation was very popular; Milton certainly studied it in his youth and was influenced by Sylvester's diction. Dryden confessed that he once preferred Sylvester to Spenser.

tresses like the morn; an echo of Homer's phrase "the fair-tressed morn," εὐπλόκαμος Ἠώς. Cf. Spenser, *Virgil's Gnat,* IX., "And fayre Aurora, with her rosie heare"(=hair). See Shelley's *Adonais,* XIV.

756—761. Spoken aside.

to have unlocked. Elizabethan writers often use this perfect infinitive "after verbs of *hoping, intending,* or verbs signifying that something *ought* to *have* been done but was not...The same idiom is found in Latin poetry after verbs of *wishing* and *intending*" (Abbott). Cf. *Par. Lost,* I. 40, "He trusted to have equalled the Most High."

759. *obtruding,* thrusting before me. *pranked,* decked. A common word in old writers; see G. Shelley has it more than once, e.g. in *The Question,* "There grew broad flag flowers, purple pranked with white."

760. *bolt;* probably a metaphor from the preparation of flour, in which to *bolt* (more correctly *boult*) is to sift the meal from the bran. Cf. the description of Coriolanus (III. 1. 322, 323) as a rough warrior not schooled

"In bolted language; meal and bran together
He throws without distinction."

Having this sense 'to refine, to sift,' the verb came by a natural metaphor to be used of subtle arguing. So we might paraphrase: 'I hate to see Vice picking out her subtle arguments while Virtue is tongue-tied and unable to check her proud enemy.'

Some take *bolt*='to dart, shoot like a bolt,' i.e. arrow; cf. 445.

766, 767. Cf. *Il Penseroso,* 46, "Spare Fast, that oft with gods doth diet." Comus had ridiculed sobriety of living as a mere freak—cf. "pet of temperance," 721; she replies that temperance is a holy, beneficent power.

767—774. Milton has in mind Gloucester's argument in

favour of practical socialism, *King Lear*, IV. I. 73, 74, viz. that Providence should make "the *superfluous* man" (cf. 773), i.e. him who has more wealth than he needs, give up part of it to his poor neighbours :

> "So distribution should undo excess,
> And each man have enough."

Lear expresses the same thought earlier, III. 4, 33—36.

Throughout this speech the real speaker is obviously Milton himself. Much of it is inappropriate in the mouth of a young girl. It should be observed that lines 779—806 (from "Shall I go on" to "more strongly") are wanting in the *Cambridge* and *Bridgewater MSS.*, i.e. the passage was added by Milton to bring out the moral of the Masque. He may have thought that there was no likelihood of *Comus* being *acted* again, and that the incongruity between the youthful speaker and her speech would be less apparent in reading the poem.

773. *unsuperfluous*, not superabundant.

774. Understand *would be. store*, abundance. She is answering Comus's argument in 728—731; cf. "cumbered," 730.

781. *contemptuous words ;* cf. 737, 738. She deals with Comus's points in turn: first temperance, then Nature's excess, then chastity.

782. *sun-clad*, radiant, lustrous; cf. 425. There is perhaps a glance at *Revelation* xii. 1: "And there appeared a great wonder in heaven; a woman clothed with the sun."

784—787. Editors quote Milton's description in the *Apology for Smectymnuus* of his early studies : "Thus, from the laureat fraternity of poets, riper years and the ceaseless round of study and reading led me to the shady spaces of philosophy; but chiefly to the divine volumes of Plato, and his equal Xenophon: where, if I should tell ye what I learnt of chastity and love, I mean that which is truly so, whose *charming cup is* only virtue, which she bears in her hand to those who are worthy; (the rest are cheated with *a thick intoxicating potion, which a certain sorceress, the abuser of love's name, carries about ;*) and how the first and chiefest office of love begins and ends in the soul, producing those happy twins of her divine generation, knowledge and virtue: with such abstracted sublimities as these, it might be worth your listening, readers," *P. W.* III. 119—121. So in the same treatise : "Having had the doctrine of Holy Scripture, unfolding those chaste and *high mysteries* with timeliest care infused, that 'the body is for the Lord'." The verbal resemblances indicate that Milton in writing these sentences recollected his earlier vindication of the "serious doctrine of Virginity." Cf. also 525, 526.

784. *Thou hast nor ear.* Cf. 997. Comus cannot hear, or hearing will not understand, her praise of purity, just as in *Arcades*, 72, 73, "the gross unpurged ear" of humanity may not catch the sound of the music from the spheres.

785. *notion*, idea, or perhaps doctrine.

mystery; used in its Scriptural sense of a truth specially revealed to men (=Gk. μυστήριον). Cf. 1 *Cor.* ii. 7, "we speak the wisdom of God in a mystery, even the hidden wisdom."

788. *art worthy*, dost deserve, in a bad sense. A rare use, but cf. *The Winter's Tale*, II. 3. 109, "worthy to be hanged."

790. *dear*, i.e. to Comus—of which he is so proud.

gay, i.e. in appearance ('showy') rather than in spirit; cf. "dazzling," 791.

791. *fence;* cf. the phrases 'to fence with a question,' and 'to parry' it, i.e. not answer it straightforwardly.

792. *convinced*, proved to be in the wrong, refuted. Cf. *Job* xxxii. 12, "behold, there was none of you that convinced Job, or that answered his words."

793. *uncontrolled*, uncontrollable, i.e. irresistible; cf. "uncontrolled tide," *Lucrece*, 645. See note on 349.

794. *rapt;* see G.

797. *brute*, dull, unsympathising; the *bruta tellus* of Horace, *Odes*, I. xxxiv. 9. Cf. Tennyson, *In Memoriam*, CXXVII., "The brute earth lightens to the sky."

her nerves, her strength; the sinews (see 660, note) being regarded as the seat of strength.

798. *thy magic structures;* Comus's "stately palace."

801. *set off;* properly 'shown to the best advantage,' as a jewel by its setting: hence 'improved by,' and so 'made more forcible,' as here.

800—806. An aside.

802—805. i.e. a shudder of horror comes upon me, though not mortal, like that which comes upon Saturn's followers when Jove thunders in his wrath and dooms them to be chained in the lowest hell.

803.   *the wrath of Jove*, the wrathful Jove ; an abstract turn of phrase imitated from the Latin.

804.   *Speaks thunder and chains ;* another classical turn of phrase, the verb being used literally with the first noun (='thunders') and figuratively with the second (='sentences them to imprisonment'). This double use of a verb is the figure of speech called *zeugma* ('a joining').

Erebus, Gk. ἔρεβος, darkness; a region of utter darkness in the nether world.

805.   *Saturn*, the Latin god *Saturnus* identified with Gk. *Cronus*. The legend was that at one time Cronus and the Titans ruled in Olympus, till Zeus (having obtained thunder and lightning from the Cyclops) hurled them into the nether world, and ruled instead. The warfare (*Titano-machia*) of the gods and Titans is often referred to in classical writers, and is to some extent the model followed by Milton in describing in *Paradise Lost* the downfall of Satan and his followers.

I must dissemble. This hackneyed phrase occurs in Marlowe's *Jew of Malta*, IV.; cf. also 2 *Henry VI.* v. 1. 13.

808.   *the canon laws of our foundation*, the fixed rules and regulations of our establishment (or institution). An allusion to the technical phrase *canon law*="ecclesiastical law as laid down in decrees of the Pope and statutes of Councils"—*Dr Murray.*

Warton notes that Milton in his prose tracts uses *canon* in contemptuous combinations: e.g. "canon iniquity'; "an insulting and only canon-wise prelate." To the Puritan poet anything suggestive of Catholicism was distasteful. Gk. κανών =rule.

The same sarcastic purpose is seen in Milton's applying the terms "consistory" (*Par. Regained*, I. 42) and "conclave" (*Par. Lost*, I. 795) to the assembly of the evil angels : the former word being specially used of the council-chamber of the Pope and the Cardinals, and the latter of the meeting at which the Cardinals elect a Pope. Perhaps a similar sneer underlies "pontifical" in *Par. Lost*, X. 313.

foundation; spoken as though Comus represented some religious institution. "God save the foundation" is Dogberry's petition, *Much Ado About Nothing*, v. 1. 327, that being the form of thanks usual among those who received alms at the door of a monastery—*Schmidt.*

809, 810. "Ancient physicians recognised four *Cardinal Humours*, viz. blood, choler, phlegm and melancholy (black bile), regarded by them as determining, by their conditions and proportions, a person's physical and mental qualities and dispositions" (*Century Dictionary*). This old physiology of the 'humours' is often alluded to by Milton; cf. *Samson Agonistes*, 600, and *Par. Lost*, XI. 543—546; in each passage he speaks of depression of spirits as caused by the black bile or humour (=*melancholy* from Gk. μέλας, black + χολή, bile). There is much on the subject in Burton's *Anatomy of Melancholy*.

812, 813. The alliteration is remarkable.

814. If the "false enchanter" had not escaped there would have been no place for Sabrina, whom Milton introduces of course out of compliment to his audience.

815. Cf. 653, "seize his wand."

816, 817. i.e. incantations spoken backwards which are potent in breaking a spell. "As old as the belief in magic itself seems to have been the belief that the effects of enchantment could be undone by reversing the spell, pronouncing the words of charm backward etc...Mesmerists now reverse their 'passes' to restore their patients"—*Masson*. In *The Faerie Queene* Britomart frees Amoret by forcing the enchanter "his charmes back to reverse" (III. 12. 36).

822. *Melibœus*, another pastoral name in classical poetry, e.g. of one of the shepherds in Vergil's first *Eclogue*; the second part of the word seems connected with βοῦς, an ox. There is thought to be a sly allusion here to Geoffrey of Monmouth, the Chronicler whose account of Sabrina Milton followed, but who was not the "soothest," i.e. most trustworthy, of writers. The reference would be parallel to Spenser's mentioning Chaucer under the pastoral pseudonym *Tityrus*. See *The Shepheards Calender, Februarie*, 92, 93, with the *Glosse*.

823. *soothest*, truest; see G.

824—842. For the Story of Sabrina see *Appendix*.

825. *sways*, rules; cf. 18, 19. *curb;* cf. "bridle in," 887.

830. *stepdame;* not strictly accurate. But it is a very artistic inaccuracy because it suggests a cause of hostility between Guendolen and Sabrina other than the real cause, and dissociates the "guiltless damsel" from her guilty mother Estrildis, whom the poet purposely omits.

834. *pearled*, adorned with pearl, which is so frequently associated with the deities of river or sea. Thus a stage direction in Ben Jonson's *Masque of Blackness* tells us that the nymphs wore on "the front, ear, necks and wrists, ornament of the most choice and orient pearl." Doubtless Sabrina and her water-nymphs would be adorned thus when they appear later on. Pearls are found in many parts of Great Britain; particularly in some of the Welsh rivers, e.g. the Esk and Conway.—*Streeter*.

835. *Nereus*, the father of the Nereids, dwelling at the bottom of the sea. Leaf remarks that he appears in Homer as πατὴρ γέρων and ἅλιος γέρων ('old man of the sea'), but is never mentioned by name. "The epithets given him by the poets refer to his *old age, his kindliness*, and his trustworthy knowledge of the future"—*Classical Dictionary*. Cf. Vergil's *grandævus Nereus* ("*aged* Nereus"), *Georgics*, IV. 392.

836. *reared*, raised; rather a favourite word with Milton. *lank*, drooping; A.-S. *hlanc*, 'bending.'

837. *his daughters;* the 50 sea-nymphs called Nereids.

838. i.e. vessels into which nectar (or liquid fragrant as nectar) had been poured and in which asphodel flowers were floating.

lavers; see Glossary, and cf. *Samson Agonistes*, 1727, 1728:

"With lavers pure, and cleansing herbs, wash off
The clotted gore."

nectared; cf. 479. *asphodil;* a plant of the lily genus, its commonest varieties being the yellow and the white ('King's Spear'). It is one of the favourite flower-names in poetry, from the classical legend that the Elysian fields were covered with 'Asphod*el*' (the modern form of the name).

839. Clearly a reminiscence of *Hamlet*, I. 5. 63, 64:
"And in the porches of mine ears did pour
The leperous distilment."

840. The editors find here echoes of the *Iliad;* e.g. of XIX. 38, where Thetis anoints the dead body of Patroclus; and XXIII. 186, where Aphrodite performs a similar office (and "ambrosial" is said of the olive oil used).

841. i.e. a change that quickly made her immortal; cf. "goddess," 842.

842. This idea of a river having a tutelary deity who dwelt in and ruled over it is essentially classical.

845. *Helping*, remedying. *urchin blasts.* Usually *urchin* signifies a hedgehog, but from the belief that evil spirits sometimes took the form of a hedgehog, *urchin* came to mean a sprite or wicked elf. Cf. *The Merry Wives of Windsor*, IV. 4. 49, "Like urchins, ouphs and fairies." So *urchin blasts* = mildew upon corn, diseases in cattle, etc., sent by evil spirits. From *urchin* = 'imp' comes the sense 'small boy.' Lat. *ericius*, a hedgehog.

ill-luck signs. For the typical tricks played by fairies see *L' Allegro*, 101—104, and *A Midsummer-Night's Dream*, II. 1. 32—57, where Puck (Robin Goodfellow) is described as a "*shrewd* and knavish sprite." Cf. also Edgar's account in *King Lear*, III. 4. 123, of the "foul fiend."

846. *the;* as if he had some particular elf in view; probably Robin Goodfellow, the influence of *A Midsummer-Night's Dream* on Milton being so strong. *shrewd*, wicked, mischievous ; see G.

848. *the shepherds at their festivals;* cf. 171—177.

850. A recognised method in pastoral verse of showing gratitude. Cf. Phineas Fletcher, *Piscatorie Eclogues*, II. 8 (speaking of the river Cam) :

" Ungrateful Chame ! how oft thy Thyrsis crown'd
  With songs and garlands thy obscurer head."

851. Cf. *Lyc.* 144. *daffodil;* see G.

852. *the old swain;* Melibœus (822). What follows was an addition by Milton to the account of the Chronicler.

Song; a solo, sung by Lawes.

862. No doubt, when Sabrina rises later on she wears a chaplet of lilies and other water-flowers.

863. *amber-dropping*, i.e. wet with the amber-coloured water of the river. Compare *Par. Lost*, III. 359, where the River of Bliss "Rolls o'er Elysian flowers her amber stream"; and Gray's *Progress of Poesy*, II. 3, "Mæander's amber waves." Exactly similar is Horace's phrase 'the yellow Tiber,' *vidimus flavum Tiberim* (*Od.* I. 2. 13), and in Matthew Arnold's *Sohrab and Rustum*, "The yellow Oxus." In these cases the adjective certainly adds to the picturesqueness of the narrative; and it may be literally true, because the tint of the river is affected by the soil of the land through which it flows. Of course, Sabrina herself will have amber hair to symbolise the river-waves.

Some editors take *amber=ambergris* (the perfume), as in *Samson Agonistes*, 720, and compare 105, 106.

dropping. It has been objected that Sabrina is still *beneath* the water, where there could not be "drops"; but the general sense may be simply 'wet, dripping with.'

865. *lake;* a complimentary description of the broad Severn. Cf. *lacus* used of the Tiber in *Æneid*, VIII. 74.

867. Note that, as Sabrina is a river-goddess, the invocation mentions only deities of the waters, and that each is described in terms taken direct from the classics, more especially from Homer. It may seem a little inappropriate that a British river-nymph should be associated so closely with Greek and Latin divinities, but Milton has forestalled the objection by placing "this Isle" (Britain) under the charge of the classical deity Neptune and his "tributary gods" (18—29).

868. *In name of*, i.e. we implore you in the name of. These lines (867—889) are the "adjuring verse" (858).

great Oceanus. The god of the river Oceanus supposed by the ancients to encircle the world; called "the Atlantic *stream*" in 97, the epithet 'Atlantic' being applied in classical writers to this great river or sea of the west. He is addressed first as being "the father of all streams," *Iliad*, XIV. 245. *great.* The epithets applied to him in the *Iliad* emphasise his power; cf. XXI. 195: "the great strength of deep-flowing Ocean, from whom all rivers flow."

869. *earth-shaking.* In Homer, the Greek god of the sea, Poseidon, is 'the earth-shaker' (κινητὴρ γᾶς, ἐννοσίγαιος, ἐνοσί χθων), "either because he is the lord of earthquakes or simply because the waves of the sea are for ever beating the land"— *Leaf.* Neptune being identified in the Roman poets with the Greek deity, "all the attributes of the latter are transferred to the former"—*Classical Dictionary.*

mace, i.e. the trident (27) which he used as sceptre. For *mace=* 'sceptre' cf. *Henry V.* IV. 1. 278, "the mace, the crown imperial."

870. "*Tethys*, the wife of Oceanus, and mother of the gods (see *Iliad*, XIV. 201), may well be supposed to have *a grave, majestic pace*, and Hesiod calls her *the venerable Tethys;* Theogony, 368"—*Newton.*

871. *hoary ..wrinkled;* cf. "*aged* Nereus," 835.

872. Referring to Proteus. *Carpathian;* he dwelt in the isle of *Carpathos,* between Rhodes and Crete. *wizard;* he had the power of foreseeing events and of changing his shape (hence *Protean* = shifting, changeable). Homer calls him "infallible" (νημερτής) and "that ancient one of the magic arts" (*Odyssey,* IV. 349, 460). *hook,* i.e. shepherd's hook (cf. *Lyc.* 120), because Proteus was shepherd of the flocks (seals) of Poseidon.

873. *Triton;* he acted as the trumpeter or herald of the marine deities, summoning or dismissing their assemblies with his "winding shell" (*concha*) or trumpet. In the lower part of his body he resembled a fish: hence "scaly." *winding* = 'crooked,' 'curling;' cf. Wordsworth's line, "Or hear old Triton blow his wreathèd horn," from the sonnet "The world is too much with us." But 'sounding' is a possible sense; we speak of 'winding a horn.' So Keats calls him "shell-winding Triton," *Endymion,* II. See *Lyc.* 89.

874. *Glaucus;* the Bœotian fisherman who eating of a certain herb became metamorphosed into a sea-god. He, too, like many sea-deities, possessed the gift of prophesying; hence "soothsaying" and "spell." He was associated with the expedition of the Argonauts, having built the ship Argo.

875. Milton alludes to Ino, daughter of Cadmus (*Odyssey,* V. 333—335), wife of Athamas, by whom she had two sons. Athamas in a fit of madness killed one son; she with the other plunged into the sea, and became a sea-goddess, under the name *Leucothea* (λευκός, white + θεά, a goddess).

"She, being *Leucothea* or the *white goddess,* may well be supposed to have *lovely hands,* which I presume the poet mentioned in opposition to Thetis' *feet* afterwards"—*Newton.* There is, indeed, a direct allusion to her hands in *Odyssey,* V. 462.

876. *her son;* Melicertes; after his deification he was called Palæmon, whom the Romans identified with Portumnus, the god of harbours (Lat. *portus,* a harbour).

877. *Thetis;* one of the Nereids, wife of Peleus and mother of Achilles.

tinsel-slippered, with flashing feet; a variation of Homer's epithet for Thetis, viz. ἀργυροπέζα, 'silver-footed,' which Milton perhaps avoided using because it had become hackneyed.

Browne had already written in *Britannia's Pastorals*, book II :

"When Triton's trumpet (with a shrill command)
Told silver-footed Thetis was at hand";

and Ben Jonson had used *silver-footed* more than once in his Masques (e.g. in *Neptune's Triumph* and *Pan's Anniversary*). *Tinsel* suggests a silvery, flashing surface, such as that of the shining cloth called *tinsel*, to which the Elizabethans often refer. Hero's wedding-dress in *Much Ado About Nothing*, III. 4. 22, was trimmed with tinsel. F. *étincelle*, a spark.

879. *Parthenope;* one of the Sirens (cf. 253); said to have been buried at Naples. Her name occurs as a synonym of Naples. Thus Wordsworth, in the fine sonnet composed on the eve of Scott's voyage to Italy, writes

" Be true,
Ye winds of ocean, and the midland sea,
Wafting your charge to soft Parthenope."

So in Landor's *Thoughts of Fiesole*:

"Sorrento softer tale may tell,
Parthenopè sound louder shell."

880. *Ligea;* another of the Sirens ; appropriately named λιγεία = 'shrill-voiced.' The reference to her " soft alluring locks" may have been suggested by Vergil, who describes Ligea and several sea-nymphs " with their bright locks flowing over their white necks" (*Georgics*, IV. 337). Otherwise, as Masson notes, it is rather the mermaids of northern mythology who comb their tresses, like the faithless wife in Matthew Arnold's *Forsaken Merman*, and Tennyson's *Mermaid*.

881. *diamond rocks;* see 732, note.

882. *sleeking.* Cf. Tennyson's description of the shepherds tending the dead Paris, "One raised the Prince, one sleek'd the squalid hair" (*The Death of Œnone*).

883, 884. Cf. *Arcades*, 96, 97.

885. How exquisitely the double alliteration suggests the effort of rising.

heave, lift. Cf. *L'Allegro*, 145, "That Orpheus' self may heave his head." So in *Par. Lost*, I. 211; *Samson Agonistes*, 197.

886. *coral-paven.* *Paven* did not necessarily imply artificial work. The " paved fountain " in *A Midsummer-Night's Dream* II. 1. 84 was "a fountain with pebbly bottom " (Clarendon Press

ed. of that play). Here the floor of the river-bed is supposed to be of coral.

Sabrina rises. From the stage-directions in other Masques it may be inferred that the appearance of the river-goddess would be effected as in a modern theatre. Part of the centre of the stage would be displaced, and through the aperture the goddess would rise, seated in her car and surrounded by a group of nymphs in picturesque dresses. The introduction in this way of deities—especially deities of the sea or rivers—was a favourite device with Masque-writers, as it gave scope for the skill of Inigo Jones, the great architect, who often designed the scenery and stage-mechanism of Masques.

890. *rushy-fringed.* A specimen of what Earle calls the 'literary' compound; that is to say, the composite word created purely for picturesque effect and confined to literature. He notes that Milton, Keats and Tennyson are conspicuous for their use of this artifice of language. Cf. "flowery-kirtled," 254; in each the simpler compound would be with a noun, not adjective—e.g. 'rush-fringed.'

893. *agate.* Derived from the name of the river Achates in Sicily, where it is said the agate was first found.

azurn, sky-blue; see G.

894. *turkis*, turquoise; see G.

895. The line illustrates Milton's way of always correcting his work for the better. In the *Cambridge MS.* the verse runs: "That my rich wheel inlays." This is practically a repetition of the previous couplet, and we miss the pretty idea in "strays." With the cancelled line cf. *Par. Lost*, IV. 701.

897. *printless*, that leave no mark. From *The Tempest*, V. 34:

"And ye that on the sands with printless feet
Do chase the ebbing Neptune."

898. *velvet;* soft as velvet; one of the stock epithets of "poetic diction." Criticising the phrase "Idalia's velvet-green" (i.e. smooth lawn) in Gray's *Progress of Poesy*, Johnson said: "an epithet or metaphor drawn from Nature ennobles Art; an epithet or metaphor drawn from Art degrades Nature."

899. Vergil had said much the same thing of Camilla, and others have said it since.

903. The metre employed from this point to the end is

much used in the Masques of Ben Jonson and other Masque-writers; perhaps because it lent itself easily to musical recitative. Cf. many of the fairy-speeches in *A Midsummer-Night's Dream*.

904. Cf. 852, 853.

907. *unblessed*, cursed; cf. 571.

908—921. The editors have noticed here, and indeed throughout the last part of *Comus*, echoes of *The Faithful Shepherdess*. Doubtless, Milton had read Fletcher's Pastoral.

912. *fountain*, i.e. the river's source, where its water is purest.

914. *Thrice;* always a significant number.

916. Cf. "enchanted chair" in the stage direction at 658.

918. *moist*, i.e. with the "drops from her fountain pure" (912). *cold;* in antithesis to the last line ("heat"), and implying 'chaste.'

919. *his*, its. We must suppose that during lines 911—918 the Lady gradually indicates her recovery of freedom.

921. *Amphitrite;* wife of Poseidon (Neptune) and goddess of the sea. The name often stands for 'the sea.' Compare Shelley's *Lines written among the Euganean Hills:*

> "Underneath day's azure eyes
> Ocean's nursling, Venice, lies,
> Amphitrite's destined halls."

923. *Anchises' line.* The legendary genealogy being: Anchises father of Æneas; Æneas father of Ascanius; Ascanius of Silvius; Silvius of Brutus; Brutus of Locrine. Cf. 827, 828.

924—937. This invocation is in the manner of pastoral verse. In Browne's *Britannia's Pastorals*, I. 2, the friendly nymph of a stream receives the same kind of blessings. But if a river proved unkind—e.g. drowned the poet's friend—it was covered with curses. Thus we find an imprecation upon the Cam in Phineas Fletcher's *Piscatorie Eclogues*, II. 23:

> "Let never myrtle on thy banks delight—
> Let dirt and mud thy lazie waters seize,
> Thy weeds still grow, thy waters still decrease."

924. *brimmed*, full to the river's brim. Tennyson's "Brook" flows along "To join the brimming river."

927. *hills.* The Welsh mountains where the Severn rises.

928. *singed air*, i.e. the torrid air of Midsummer when the dog-star prevails. Cf. *Lyc.* 138, note. The participle has an active force = 'singeing, i.e. scorching.'

929. *tresses;* "the foliage of the trees and shrubs along the banks"—*Dr Bradshaw.*

931. The water of the river is likened to liquefied crystal.

932. *billows.* By this time Milton has traced the Severn down to Gloucester, where it becomes an arm of the sea, and as such may be said to have 'billows.' "Severn *Sea*" is a common local name for the upper part of the Bristol Channel.

933. *beryl;* a yellow crystal. L. *beryllus* (Gk. βήρυλλος), whence F. *briller*=to sparkle like a beryl.

934. I think now that *lofty head* must be taken literally of the river's *source* contrasted with its *banks* (936)—the general sense being, 'May many a tower and terrace (i.e. some great city) encircle, like a crown, your source in the Welsh hills, and may groves adorn your banks at intervals along your course to the sea.'

Some interpret *head* of the river itself, not merely its source ; compare Dr Bradshaw's paraphrase: "May you be crowned with many a tower and terrace on your lofty sides, and here and there with groves of myrrh on the banks." But surely "on your lofty sides" is the same as "on the banks," whereas some contrast between *head* and *banks* seems to be intended.

The metaphor in 934, 935 suggests, possibly was suggested by, the phrase στεφάνωμα πύργων, 'the encircling towers,' literally 'the crown of towers' (round Thebes), in the *Antigone*, 121, of Sophocles. Here the metaphor gains appropriateness from the fact that the river is personified as a maiden.

936, 937. Strictly dependent on the construction in 934, 935, i.e. 'and may thy head be crowned with groves upon thy banks.' But from *thy head* we can easily supply *thou*='mayst *thou* be crowned with groves upon thy banks.'

937. The landscape is obviously ideal, "groves of myrrh and cinnamon" being common enough in the land of poetic fancy, but not found in the West of England.

942. *waste,* unnecessary ; cf. "waste fertility," 729.

945. *this gloomy covert,* i.e. the wood in which the "stately palace" of Comus lay. Either the scene is still in this palace, but the stage is so arranged that the wood can be seen outside ; or there has been some change of scenery so as to represent the original wood again instead of the interior of the palace.

949. *gratulate,* welcome; cf. "And gratulate his safe return to Rome," *Titus Andronicus,* I. 221.

then come in Country Dancers. Technically this is the second *Anti-masque;* the first being the "monstro is rout" at line 92.

958, 959. A variation on *L'Allegro,* 97, 98.

960. i.e. not in the rude style of a peasants' dance.

962. *court guise,* i.e. an elegant bearing such as befits a dance like the *pavane* or *minuet.*

964. *mincing,* moving with dainty steps ; F. *mince,* 'dainty, neat.' Editors refer to *Isaiah* iii. 16. *Dryades*=wood-nymphs ; from δρῦς, an oak. With the rhyme, cf. *Lyc.* 154—156.

965. *lawns;* see 568.

Song. No doubt there were dances ("other trippings ") before and after it. Characters not named would take part in them, as well as the Lady, the two Brothers and the Spirit.

966. For the actors to come forward and address some member, or members, of the audience was not unusual in Masques. Thus in Shirley's *Triumph of Peace* the chorus twice advance to the front of the stage and salute the king and queen.

970 *timely,* early; as always in Shakespeare; cf. *The Comedy of Errors,* I. I. 139, "happy were I in my timely death."

972. *assays,* trials, tests ; see G.

976—980. The metrical and general resemblance of these verses to *The Tempest,* V. I (" Where the bee sucks "), has often been noticed. It is to me clear that from line 976 to the close Milton's conception of the Attendant Spirit owed much to Shakespeare's Ariel, and to Puck in *A Midsummer-Night's Dream.* As already explained, the Epilogue spoken at the actual performance of *Comus* began at line 1012. Lines 976—1011 had been used at the outset.

976. *the ocean;* the regular classical term for the great sea of the west (the Atlantic) in which tradition placed the "happy isles...thrice happy isles" (*Par. Lost* III. 567) containing the Gardens of the Hesperides.

977—979. i.e. those happy regions where the sun ever shines in the broad heaven.

clime; see G. 'Eye of day, or heaven' is a favourite phrase for the sun in Elizabethan poetry. Cf. Milton's Sonnet to the nightingale, "Thy liquid notes that close the eye of day." Line 979 is practically from Vergil, *Æneid,* VI. 887.

980. *There;* in those "happy climes." *liquid,* clear, brilliant (Lat. *liquidus*).

982. *Hesperus;* see 393—396, note.

983. *golden;* transferred from the apples to the tree itself.

984. *crisped,* i.e. by the wind ruffling the leaves; more often applied to a breeze stirring the surface of water, as in *Childe Harold* IV. 211, "I would not their vile breath should crisp the stream."

985. *spruce,* dainty, prettily adorned, i.e. with flowers etc.

986. *Graces,* Lat. *Gratiæ,* Gk. χάριτες; three goddesses (Euphrosyne, Aglaia, Thalia) who personified the refinements and elevated joys of life.

Hours, Lat. *Horæ,* Gk. ὧραι; goddesses personifying the seasons of the year; the course of the seasons was symbolically described as "the dance of the *Horæ*" (cf. *Par. Lost,* V. 394, 395). Classical writers often mention them along with the Graces. The Graces and Hours were favourite allegorical *dramatis personæ* in Masques.

rosy-bosomed; Gk. ῥοδόκολπος. Cf. Gray, *Ode on the Spring,*
"Lo! where the rosy-bosom'd Hours,
   Fair Venus' train, appear";
and Thomson, "the rose-bosomed Spring" (*Spring,* 1010).

A very notable feature of English poetry from the Restoration to (about) the French Revolution, i.e. during the period beginning with Dryden and ending with Johnson (died 1784), is the great influence of the diction of Milton's poems, *especially* the minor poems. In Dryden and Pope, Collins and Gray and Thomson, and the minor writers, we are struck by constant echoes of *L'Allegro and Il Penseroso, Lycidas* and *Comus*— thanks, no doubt, to their extreme verbal felicity, their fulfilment of Coleridge's definition of poetry as the right words in the right places.

989. *west winds,* the 'Zephyrs' of classical poetry; traditionally the fragrance-laden winds; cf. again Gray's *Ode on the Spring:*
"While, whisp'ring pleasure as they fly,
   Cool Zephyrs thro' the clear blue sky
   Their gather'd fragrance fling."

990. *cedarn alleys,* paths bordered by cedar trees. *cedarn;* formed from the noun, i.e. *cedar-n,* like *silver-n, leather-n.*

Now purely poetic; cf. Matthew Arnold, *The New Sirens*, "The slumb'rous cedarn shade."

991. Cf. "All thy garments smell of myrrh, and aloes, and cassia," *Psalm* xlv. 8.

nard, spikenard (i.e. spiked nard, *nardus spicatus*), a fragrant Indian root. The word comes from Sanskrit *nal*, to smell. Probably the Jews got the perfume and its name through the Persians. *cassia*, a spice of the nature of cinnamon, as in the Bible. *Cassia* is now used of an extract of laurel-bark.

992. *Iris*; the goddess of the rainbow (cf. "bow") and messenger of the gods, especially of Juno. Cf. the 'Masque' in *The Tempest*.

993. *blow*, make to bloom; rarely transitive. See *Lyc.* 48.

994—997. On the rhymes see 511, 512, note.

purpled, embroidered; see G. *Elysian*, heavenly; see 257.

997. *if your ears be true*, "i.e. if you have minds fine enough to perceive the real meaning of the legends I am about to cite"—*Masson*.

These legends of Venus and Adonis, Cupid and Psyche, have often been treated from a mundane, indeed sensual point of view; whereas we ought to see in them an elevated, spiritual significance which is hidden from those whose vision is dimmed by sin. Such seems the general bearing of the passage.

999—1002. The legend of Adonis, the youth beloved by the Greek goddess Aphrodite (=the Roman goddess Venus), was that he was killed in the chase by a wild boar, mourned for by Aphrodite, and at last, in consideration of her sorrow, suffered by the gods of the lower world to spend six months in every year upon earth with her. His yearly return to earth was celebrated by religious rites such as Theocritus describes in the xvth *Idyl*. Usually the legend is explained as being a symbolisation of the annual return of spring: "in the Asiatic religions Aphrodite was the fructifying principle of nature, and Adonis appears to have reference to the death of nature in winter and its revival in spring—hence he spends six months in the lower and six in the upper world"—*Classical Dictionary*. In fact Adonis was regarded as the god of the Solar year.

The story is of Phœnician origin, Adonis being the same as Tammuz ('Sun of Life') mentioned in *Ezekiel* viii. 14, "behold, there sat women weeping for Tammuz." See the fuller reference in *Par. Lost*, I. 446—452, and *Nativity Ode*, 204, "In vain the *Tyrian* [Phœnician] maids their *wounded Thammuz* mourn."

His yearly six months on earth were supposed to be spent in the 'Garden of Adonis,' which became a synonym of an exquisitely lovely spot like the Garden of Eden. The chief reference to it in the classics is in Pliny's *Natural History*, XIX. 4. The allusion is a favourite with poets. See *Par. Lost*, IX. 439, 440; I *Henry VI*. I. 6. 7; Spenser's *Hymne in Honour of Love*, 22—28; Keats's *Endymion*, II.; and above all, *The Faerie Queene*, III. 6. 29—49, which Milton had undoubtedly in his thoughts here. For like Milton Spenser treats the story as an allegory of the immortality of love and says (III. 6. 46—48) that after his restoration to life Aphrodite would not let Adonis descend to the nether world but kept him in the 'Garden.'

Milton has not, I believe, any classical authority for associating the Gardens of Adonis and of the *Hesperides*, but his purpose here is to bring together all the most beautiful things in nature of which classical legend tells, and thus form an ideal region, a paradise of perfect loveliness. And he exercises the privilege of making the classics serve his poetic purpose.

Lines 999—1002 remind us of Tennyson's picture in the *Palace of Art* of King Arthur after his "passing" to the island-valley:

"Or mythic Uther's deeply-wounded son
    In some fair space of sloping greens
    Lay, dozing in the vale of Avalon,
        And watch'd by weeping queens."

1000.   *Waxing*, growing. Cf. Germ. *wachsen*, to grow.

1002.   *the Assyrian queen*, i.e. Aphrodite, whose "worship was of Eastern origin, and probably introduced by the Phœnicians to the islands of Cyprus, Cythera and others, from whence it spread all over Greece. She appears to have been originally identical with Astarte, called by the Hebrews Ashtoreth, and her connection with Adonis clearly points to Syria"—*Classical Dictionary*. Identical with the *Assyrian* goddess *Istar*.

1003—1011.   He passes to a yet more spiritual love: not on earth, as that of Adonis and Aphrodite, but in heaven itself.

The myth of Psyche is an allegory of the human soul (ψυχή) which, after undergoing trials and tortures, is purified by pain and eventually reaches happiness and rest. Milton wished to emphasize the sanctity of love still more, by showing that there is a place for it among the gods. "Comus," says Masson, "had misapprehended Love, knew nothing of it except its vile counterfeit...had been outwitted and defeated. But there *is* true Love, and it is to be found in Heaven." The idea is well illustrated by *Par. Lost*, VIII. 615—629, where Adam questions the archangel Raphael—"Love not the Heavenly Spirits?"—and receives the reply—"without Love no happiness."

No doubt Milton was influenced by that conception of Divine Love of which Plato treats in the *Phædrus* and elsewhere. The story of Cupid and Psyche is applied in much the same way by Spenser, *The Faerie Queene*, III. 6. 49, 50. See also Keats's *Ode to Psyche*.

1003. Cf. *Midsummer-Night's Dream*, II. 1. 29, "By fountain clear or spangled starlight sheen." *sheen;* akin to Germ. *schön*, beautiful.

1004. *advanced*, raised aloft.

1011. *Youth and Joy.* Later in life Milton made Virtue and Knowledge the offspring of pure Love; see note on 784 —787. "Editors find a reason for this in the greater gravity of spirit which eight years had brought upon Milton"—*Masson*.

1012. A series of reminiscences of Shakespeare; cf. *A Midsummer-Night's Dream*, IV. 1. 102, 103, where Oberon says: "We the globe can compass soon;" and II. 1. 175, Puck's words, "I'll put a girdle round about the earth," i.e. make the circuit of the universe; and *Macbeth*, III. 5. 23, 24:

"Upon the corner of the moon

There hangs a vaporous drop profound."
There and here (1017) *corner*='horn' (Lat. *cornu*), as in *cornua lunæ*; cf. Vergil's third *Georgic*, 433.

1014. *the green earth's end;* meaning probably the Cape Verd Islands—*Sympson*. Cf. *Par. Lost*, VIII. 631, "Beyond the Earth's green Cape and verdant Isles." They or the Canaries were commonly identified by the Elizabethans with the classical *Hesperidum 'Insulæ*.

1015. *bowed*, because in any landscape the horizon appears to come down to the earth. *welkin;* see G. *slow*, i.e. gradually.

1018—1023. These lines are particularly notable as summing up the whole teaching of the poem. The special aspect of virtue which it has depicted is, of course, "saintly chastity" (453).

And chastity (the Lady) has triumphed over the temptations of intemperance (Comus), through its own "hidden strength" (418), and through supernatural aid (the Attendant Spirit and Sabrina) such as the Elder Brother spoke of (455, 456) and the last line of the Masque promises.

1019. Ben Jonson's *Pleasure Reconciled to Virtue* (the Masque in which Comus appears) ends with a similar song in praise of Virtue.

1021. *sphery clime.* An allusion to the notion, said to have originated with Pythagoras and described by Plato in the *Republic* (x. 616, 617), of the "music of the spheres." As *popularly* understood and referred to, it was that the rapid revolution of each planet in its "sphere" or orbit (i.e. a circular space round the central earth) produced a sound, and the combination of the sounds a harmony. Poetry is full of allusions to "the great sphere-music of stars and constellations" (Tennyson, *Parnassus*). It was a favourite idea with Milton, who studied the Ptolemaic theory of the "spheres" deeply, and adopted it for the astronomical system of *Par. Lost.* Cf. *The Nativity Ode*, 125—132, Ode *At a Solemn Music*, and *Arcades*, 62—73. Perhaps Echo was called "Daughter of the sphere" (241) in allusion to the music of the spheres, i.e. as though she had her origin in it and were part of it.

sphery, belonging to the spheres.

1023, 1024. Masson notes that an interesting personal anecdote is associated with these lines, viz. that Milton wrote them, and his name, in the autograph-book (still preserved) of a foreigner whom he visited in June 1639 at Geneva, on the way home from his travels in Italy.

The peaceful close of *Comus* is characteristic of Milton. All his long poems end quietly. Indeed, the end of *Paradise Lost* is so simple that some critics proposed, wrongly, to omit the last couplet as unauthentic because tame and less impressive than the two previous lines. But it is just like the gentle ending of *Paradise Regained.* Shakespeare's tragedies usually close on a quiet note.

GLOSSARY.

Abbreviations:—

A.S. = Anglo-Saxon, i.e. English down to about the Conquest.

Middle E. = Middle English, i.e. English from about the Conquest to about 1500.

Elizabethan E. = the English of Shakespeare and his contemporaries (down to about 1650).

O.F. = Old French, i.e. till about 1600.   F. = modern French.

Germ. = modern German.   Gk. = Greek.

Ital. = Italian.   Lat. = Latin.

NOTE: In using the Glossary the student should pay very careful attention to the context in which each word occurs.

alabaster, *Com.* 660, sulphate of lime; Gk. ἀλάβαστρος, said to be derived from the name of a town, *Alabastron*, in Egypt. Misspelt *alablaster* in the original editions, as commonly in Elizabethan writers.

alley, 'a path, walk,' especially one with trees overhead (*Com.* 311), as in a garden (990). Cf. *Much Ado About Nothing*, I. 2. 10, "a thick-pleached alley," i.e. thickly interwoven overhead; and Tennyson, *Ode to Memory*, "plaited alleys of the trailing rose." F. *allée*.

ambrosial; used by Milton of that which delights the sense of smell (*Com.* 16, 840) or taste. Strictly, *ambrosia* = the food of the gods, as *nectar* = their drink.

aspect, *Com.* 694. Shakespeare always accents *aspéct*. Many words now accented on the first syllable were in

Elizabethan E. accented on the second syllable, i.e. they re-tained the French accent, which (roughly speaking) was that of the original Latin words. By "accent" one means, of course, the stress laid by the voice on any syllable in pronouncing it. Thus Milton wrote "By policy and long *procéss* of time" (*Par. Lost*, II. 297); cf. French *procès*, Lat. *procéssus*. So Shakespeare scans *accéss*, *commérce*, *edíct*, when it suits him.

asphodil, *Com.* 838; Gk. ἀσφόδελος, a kind of lily supposed to flourish especially in the Elysian fields. **Daffodil** (*Com.* 851) is a corruption of ἀσφόδελος through Low Lat. *affodillus;* now used of a different flower, viz. the *pseudo-narcissus*. Skeat thinks that the *d* may represent F. *de* in *fleur d'affrodille*.

assay, *Com.* 972, 'trial, test.' The form always used by Milton. To *assay* metals is to test them. Cf. O.F. *essai* and the variant form *assai;* Lat. *exagium*, 'a weighing, trial of weight.'

ay me, *Com.* 511, 'alas.' O.F. *aymi*, 'alas for me!' cf. Gk. οἴμοι.

azurn, *Com.* 893; perhaps formed from the noun *azure*, like *silvern* from *silver*, where *-n* = the suffix *-en*, as in *wooden*, *woollen*. Some think that Milton, with his fondness for Italian, coined *azurn* from Ital. *azzurrino*. Instances of his leaning towards half Italian forms are *sdein* (Ital. *sdegnare*), *serenate* (Ital. *serenata*), *sovran*, *harald* (Ital. *araldo*). See *Par. Lost*, I. 752, II. 518, IV. 50, 769.

balm; properly the aromatic oily resin of the *balsam*-tree: then any fragrant oil or ointment for anointing, soothing pain, and so any fragrant or soothing liquid (as in *Com.* 674). Hence **balmy** = 'fragrant' (*Com.* 991).

be. The root *be* was conjugated in the present tense in-dicative, singular and plural, up till about the middle of the 17th century. The singular, indeed, was almost limited in Elizabethan E. to the phrase "if thou *beest*," where the in-dicative *beest* has the force of the subjunctive; cf. *The Tempest*, V. 134, "if thou be'st Prospero." For the plural cf. *Genesis* xlii. 32, "We be twelve brethren," and *Matthew* xv. 14, "they be blind leaders of the blind."

blank, *Com.* 452, 'dismayed.' Cf. the verb *blank* = 'to confound' in *Samson Agonistes*, 471, literally 'to make to *blanch* or *blench*, i.e. become white' (F. *blanc*).

bolt, or **boult**, *Com.* 760, 'to sift, refine.' O.F. *buleter*, a corruption of *bureter*, 'to sift through coarse red cloth' (Low Lat. *burra*, '*red* cloth,' from the root of Gk. πῦρ, 'fire'). For *r* softening into *l* in French cf. 'pé*l*erin,' 'a pilgrim,' Lat. 'peregrinus.'

bosky, *Com.* 313, 'covered with bushes, shrubs'; *bosk* (whence *bosk-y*, like *bush-y* from *bush*) meant a bush or clump of bushes. Cognate with *bush*, *bouquet*, F. *bois*, 'wood.'

bourn, *Com.* 313, 'a brook'; the same as north-country *burn*; akin to Germ. *brunnen*, 'a spring.' Cf. *Bourne*-mouth. Distinct from *bourn*, 'a limit' (F. *borne*).

brinded, *Com.* 443; an older form than *brindled*; it means literally 'marked as with a *brand*,' and generally indicates stripes of dark colour on the tawny coat of an animal. Cf. "the brinded cat," *Macbeth*, IV. I. I.

budge, *Com.* 707. Skeat says: "a kind of fur. *Budge* is lamb skin with the wool dressed outwards; orig. simply 'skin'—F. *bouge*, a wallet, great pouch, Lat. *bulga*, a little bag, a word of Gaulish origin." He refers to the same root the word *budget* = 'a leathern bag,' in *The Winter's Tale*, IV. 3. 20. Others connect with O.F. *bouchet*, 'a kid,' because an old writer says that *budge* was the fur of kids.

character, *Com.* 530, 'to stamp.' Gk. χαρακτήρ, 'a stamp on a coin, seal, etc., engraved mark.' For a good instance of its strict use cf. *The Faerie Queene*, V. 6. 2:

"Whose *character* in th' Adamantine *mould*
Of his true heart so firmly was *engraved*."

clime, *Com.* 977, 'land, country'; cf. 2 *Henry VI.* III. 2. 84, "Drove back again unto my native clime." Gk. κλίμα, 'a slope,' from κλίνειν, 'to slope.' *Clime* and *climate* are 'doublets,' and each meant 'region,' then 'temperature,' the most important quality of a region.

clouted, *Com.* 635, 'patched, mended'; cf. *Joshua* ix. 5, "old shoes and clouted upon their feet." A.S. *clút*, 'a patch.'

cozen, *Com.* 737. According to the common (but not certain) explanation, to *cozen* a man is to pretend to be his *cousin* for the purpose of getting something out of him: whence 'to cheat.'

curfew, *Com.* 435; literally the signal to cover up (i.e. put out) the fire—F. *couvrir* + *feu*.

discover, 'to lay open to view, reveal,' literally 'uncover,' F. *découvrir*. Often in stage-directions; cf. Ben Jonson's *Masque of Beauty*, "Here a curtain was drawn [aside] and the scene discovered."

ditty, used strictly of the words of a song (*Lyc.* 32), but in *Com.* 86 of the music; cf. **smooth-dittied** = 'with smooth-flowing air.' From Lat. *dictatum*, 'something dictated'; not from *dictum*.

faery, *Com.* 118, 435; originally a collective noun = 'fairy folk, fairy land, enchantment'; cf. the title of *The Faerie Queene*. Late Lat. *fata*, 'a fairy,' formed from the plural of *fatum*, 'fate.'

fond, *Com.* 67, 'foolish,' its old meaning. Hence **fondly** = 'foolishly' (*Lyc.* 56). Originally *fond* was the p. p. of a Middle E. verb *fonnen*, 'to act like a fool,' from the noun *fon*, 'a fool.' The root is Scandinavian.

founder; properly 'to sink to the bottom,' Lat. *fundus*; cf. F. *s'effondrer*, 'to sink.' Hence **night-foundered** = 'plunged in night' (*Com.* 483).

fraught, *Com.* 355, 'laden, filled'; the abbreviated p. p. (*fraughted* was rarely used) of the verb *fraught*, 'to load'—see *Cymbeline*, I. I. 126—which is now obsolete except in this p. p. Akin probably to *freight*.

gloze, or **glose**, *Com.* 161, 'to speak falsely, to flatter.' Middle E. *glosen* meant 'to make *glosses*, explain,' from Late Lat. *glossa*, Gk. γλῶσσα, which signified (1) the tongue, (2) a language, (3) a word, (4) an explanation of a word. The verb *glosen* got the idea 'to explain *falsely*,' whence 'to deceive.' So *glozing* = 'deceptive'; cf. George Herbert, *The Dotage*, "False glozing pleasures." Especially used of flattering, false speech.

goblin, *Com.* 436. Late Lat. *gobelinus*, a diminutive of Lat. *cobalus*, 'a mountain-sprite, demon' = Gk. κόβαλος, 'a rogue,' or 'a goblin supposed to befriend rogues.'

grain, *Com.* 750; O.F. *graine* = Low Lat. *granum*, which, like the classical Lat. *coccum* ('a berry'), was used of the scarlet dye made from the *cochineal* insect found on the scarlet oak, the insect being like a berry or seed. Properly therefore *grain* = 'scarlet hue,' but Elizabethan poets seem to use it in the extended sense 'hue, colour.' As *grain* was a very strong dye, so that the colour of cloth dyed *in grain* never washed out but seemed to be part of the texture itself, the word came to signify 'texture, fibre,' of cloth or wood. An *ingrained* fault is one that has become of the very texture of a man's character.

griesly, *Com.* 603, 'horrible'; cognate with *grucsome* and Germ. *grausig, grässlich.* Cf. *The Faerie Queene,* III. 1. 17, "Lo! where a griesly foster forth did rush" (i.e. forester).

his; this was the ordinary *neuter* (as well as masculine) possessive pronoun in Middle E. and remained so in Elizabethan E. Cf. *Genesis* iii. 15, "*it* shall bruise thy head, and thou shalt bruise *his* heel." There was also a use, not common, of *it* (Middle E. *hit*) as a possessive, though uninflected; especially in the phrase *it own.* Cf. *The Tempest,* II. 1. 163, "of it own kind," and the Bible of 1611 in *Leviticus* xxv. 5, "of it owne accord." This possessive use of *it* without *own* to strengthen it seems to have been somewhat familiar in Elizabethan E., applied especially to children; cf. *The Winter's Tale,* III. 2. 101, "The innocent milk in *it* most innocent mouth."

Then from the possessive use of *it* uninflected there arose, about the close of the 16th century, the inflected form *its* in which -*s* is the usual possessive inflection, as in *his.* This new form *its* came into use slowly, the old idiom *his* being generally retained by Elizabethans. There are no instances of *its* in Spenser or the Bible (1611), and only three in Milton's poetical works (*Paradise Lost,* I. 254, IV. 813, *Nativity Ode,* 106). *Its* does not occur in any extant work of Shakespeare printed prior to his death: hence it seems not improbable that the nine instances in the 1st Folio (five in a single play, *The Winter's Tale*) were due to the editors or printers of the Folio.

hutch, *Com.* 719, 'to enclose.' F. *huche,* 'a hutch, bin,' Low Lat. *hutica;* probably from same root as Germ. *hüten,* 'to guard.' A *bolting-hutch* is the bin into which flour is sifted.

influence, *Com.* 336; Late Lat. *influentia,* literally 'a flowing in upon' (Lat. *in + fluere*). An astrological term applied to the power over the earth, men's characters, fortunes etc., which was supposed to descend from the celestial bodies. Cf. "planetary influence," *King Lear,* I. 2. 136; "skyey influences," *Measure for Measure,* III. 1. 9. Other terms due to astrology are 'dis*aster*' (Lat. *astrum,* 'a star'), 'ill-*starred*,' 'jovial,' 'saturnine.'

inherit; then often used='to have, possess,' without (as now) the notion of '*heir*ship' (Lat. *heres,* 'an heir'). Cf.

in the Prayer-Book, "And bless thine inheritance"—that is, 'thy peculiar possession, thy people.' Hence **disinherit**, 'to make to cease to have, to dispossess' (*Com.* 334).

inure, *Com.* 735, 'to accustom,' literally 'to bring into practice' (=*ure*). For the obsolete noun *ure* (F. *œuvre*, 'work,' Lat. *opera*) cf. Bacon's Essay *Of Simulation*, "lest his hand should be out of ure," i.e. out of practice. Cf. 'man*ure*.'

laver, *Com.* 838, 'a vessel for washing'; Lat. *lavare*, 'to wash.' The *laver* mentioned in 1 *Kings* vii. 30 was a large basin in the Temple for the ablution of the priests.

lawn; properly (*Com.* 568, 965) an open grass-covered space in a wood, like the glades in the New Forest ; hence a poetical word for **any** 'pasture' (*Lyc.* 25), 'green.' Perhaps cognate with F. *lande*, 'waste land'; cf. the *landes* or waste country south of Bordeaux.

lewd, *Com.* 465; Middle E. *lewed*=A.S. *lǽwed*. Its successive meanings were: (1) 'enfeebled,' *lǽwed* (=*gelǽwed*) being the past participle of *lǽwan*, 'to weaken'; then (2) 'ignorant'; then (3) 'bad'; then (4) 'lustful,' i.e. bad in a particular way. From (2) arose also the sense 'lay, belonging to the laity,' because the laity compared with the clergy were ignorant.

lickerish, *Com.* 700, 'dainty'; something pleasant to *lick*. Cf. the cognate F. *lécher*, 'to lick'; Germ. *leckerei*, 'dainties.'

list, 'to wish, please'; commonly a present (*Lyc.* 123), rarely a preterite (*Com.* 49). Shakespeare once has *listed*; cf. *Richard III.* III. 5. 84, "his savage heart...*listed* to make his prey." Akin to *lust*, which often meant 'pleasure,' as does Germ. *lust*; cf. *Psalm* xcii. 10, "Mine eye also shall see his lust of mine enemies" (Prayer-Book).

livery, *Com.* 455; in Elizabethan E.='any kind of dress, garb'; cf. *L'Allegro*, 62, "The clouds in thousand liveries dight." Originally *livery* meant whatever was given (i.e. *delivered*) by a lord to his household, whether food, money or garments. From F. *livrer*.

lull, *Com.* 260; an imitative word formed from *lu lu* hummed by nurses in composing children to sleep. Hence *lullaby*.

madrigal, *Com.* 495; Ital. *madrigale*, 'a pastoral song,' from Gk. μάνδρα, 'a fold, stable.' The madrigal was one of the most characteristic forms of old English music.

main, *Com.* 28; Icelandic *megin*, 'mighty,' common in

compounds, e.g. *megin-sjör*, 'mighty sea'; from the same root as Gk. μέγας, Lat. *magnus:* whence also **mickle** (*Com.* 31) or *micel*, 'great,' Middle E. *michel* or *muchel* (cf. *much*).

methinks; methought, *Com.* 171, 482. These are really *impersonal* constructions such as were much used in pre-Elizabethan E.; their meaning is, 'it *seems,* or seemed, *to* me.' The pronoun is a dative, and the verb is not the ordinary verb 'to *think*'=A.S. þencan, but an obsolete impersonal verb 'to *seem*'=A.S. þyncan. These cognate verbs got confused through their similarity; the distinction between them as regards usage and sense is shown in Milton's *Paradise Regained*, II. 266, "*Him thought* he by the brook of Cherith stood"='to him it seemed that' etc. Cf. their German cognates *denken*, 'to think,' used personally, and the impersonal *es dünkt*, 'it seems'; also the double use of Gk. δοκεῖν. For the old impersonal constructions cf. Spenser, *Prothalamion* 60, "*Them seem'd* they never saw a sight so fayre."

nice; Lat. *nescius*, 'ignorant.' It first meant 'foolish,' as in Chaucer; then 'foolishly particular, fastidious, prudish' (*Com.* 139); then 'subtly,' since fastidiousness implies drawing fine, subtle distinctions. The original notion 'foolish' often affects the Elizabethan uses of the word, which is noticeable as having improved in sense.

ore, *Com.* 719, 933, 'metal'; A.S. *ór*, 'unrefined metal'; cf. Germ. *erz*. Sometimes Elizabethan writers use *ore*='gold,' i.e. through confusion of sound with Lat. *aurum*. Thus it means 'precious metal' in *Hamlet*, IV. 1. 25.

orient, 'bright, lustrous'; in Elizabethan poetry a constant epithet of gems, especially pearls. Perhaps, used thus, it first meant 'eastern,' gems coming from the Orient or East; then as these were bright it got the notion 'lustrous.' Commonly Milton applies it to liquids (*Com.* 65) or jewels; cf. "orient pearl," *Par. Lost*, V. 2.

pert, *Com.* 118. Shakespeare always uses it in a good sense='lively, alert'; cf. *A Midsummer-Night's Dream*, I. 1. 13, "Awake the pert and nimble spirit of youth." Middle E. *pert* is another form of *perk*, 'smart'; it got its bad sense 'saucy' through confusion with *malapert*, from Lat. *male+expertus*, 'too experienced,' hence 'too sharp,' 'saucy.'

pester, *Com.* 7, 'to shackle, clog.' Short for *impester*=F.

empêtrer, which "signifies properly to hobble a horse while he feeds afield"—*Brachet*; from Lat. *in*, 'on, upon'+medieval Lat. *pastorium*, 'a clog for horses at *pasture*.' From 'to shackle' follows naturally the sense 'to annoy, bother.'

pinfold, *Com.* 7, 'a pound, i.e. enclosure for strayed cattle.' Short for '*pind*-fold,' from A.S. *pyndan*, 'to *pen* up.' Cognate with *pound*. Cf. "Lipsbury pinfold," *King Lear*, II. 2. 8.

plighted, *Com.* 301, 'folded.' Spenser uses *plight*='fold' both as noun and verb; cf. *The Faerie Queene*, II. 3. 26, "many a folded plight," and VI. 7. 43, "And on his head a roll of linen plight." Cf. the cognate *plait* (or *pleat*) and F. *pli*, *plier*; all from Lat. *plicare*, 'to fold.'

prank, *Com.* 759, 'to deck, adorn'; cf. *The Winter's Tale*, IV. 4. 10, "most goddess-like pranked up." A favourite word with Herrick; cf. *The Harvest Home*, "Some prank them up with oaken leaves." Akin to *prance* (properly 'to make a show'), and Germ. *prunk*, 'pomp.'

prevent, *Com.* 285, 'to anticipate'; Lat. *prævenire*, 'to come before.' Cf. *Psalm* cxix. 148, "mine eyes prevent the night watches."

purchase, *Com.* 607, 'booty, prey.' The verb meant first to hunt after (F. *pour*+*chasser*); "then to take in hunting; then to acquire; and then, as the commonest way of acquiring is by giving money in exchange, to buy"—*Trench*. The sense 'to acquire, gain' is common in Elizabethan E. Cf. 1 *Timothy* iii. 13, "they that have used the office of a deacon well purchase to themselves a good degree" (Revised Version 'gain').

purfled, *Com.* 995, 'embroidered'; cf. *The Faerie Queene*, I. 2. 13, "Purfled with gold and pearle of rich assay." F. *pourfilé* (*fil*, 'a thread,' Lat. *filum*). The word survives in *purl*, a term used in lace-making.

quire, *Com.* 112. An older form of *choir*, Lat. *chorus*; cf. O.F. *quer* and F. *chœur*. "In Quires and places where they sing," Prayer-Book.

rapt, *Com.* 794, 'transported.' It should be written *rapped*, being the past participle of an old verb *rap*, 'to seize hurriedly'; cf. *Cymbeline*, I. 6. 51, "what...thus raps you?" i.e. what transports you thus? The form *rapt* comes through confusion with Lat. *raptus*, the p. p. of Lat. *rapere*, 'to seize.'

sad, *Com.* 189, 355, 'grave, serious,' without any notion of

sorrow. Cf. *Henry V.* IV. I. 318, "the sad and solemn priests." Originally 'sated,' A.S. *sæd* being akin to Lat. *satis*, 'enough.'

shrewd, *Com.* 846, 'malicious, mischievous'; from its common Elizabethan sense 'bad,' literally 'cursed' (*shrewd* being the p. p. of *schrewen*, 'to curse'). Cf. "a shrewd turn" = 'a bad turn,' *All's Well That Ends Well*, III. 5. 71. From *shrew* = A.S. *scredwa*, "a shrew-mouse, fabled to have a very venomous bite" (Skeat).

shroud; properly 'a garment' (A.S. *scrúd*)—cf. *Lyc.* 22; hence any 'shelter, covering,' *Com.* 147. Outside Old St Paul's Cathedral in London there was a covered place called "the Shrouds," were sermons were preached in wet weather, instead of at St Paul's Cross, which was in the open.

sooth, *Com.* 823, 'true.' A.S. *sóð*, 'true'; cf. *soothsayer*, *forsooth*.

sound, *Com.* 115, 'a strait, strip of water'; A.S. *sund*, literally 'a strait of the sea that could be *swum* across.'

sovran, *Com.* 41; spelt thus always in *Par. Lost*; cf. Ital. *sovrano*. The common form *sovereign* = O.F. *soverain*. Lat. *superanus*, 'chief,' from *super*, 'above.'

stole, *Com.* 195. Elizabethans often use the form of the past tense as a past participle—cf. **took** (*Com.* 558); and conversely with certain verbs, e.g. *begin*, *sing*, *spring*, the form of the past participle as a past tense. Thus Shakespeare and Milton nearly always use *sung* instead of *sang;* cf. *Par. Lost*, III. 18, " I *sung* of Chaos and eternal Night."

swink; A.S. *swincan*, 'to work hard, labour.' Hence the sense 'wearied with work' in *Com.* 293. A common verb in old writers; cf. *The Faerie Queene*, II. 7. 8:

"Honour, estate, and all this worldes good,
    For which men swinck and sweat incessantly."

Shelley has it in his humorous *Letter to Maria Gisborne:*

"that dew which the gnomes drink,
    When at their subterranean toil they swink."

take ; used by Elizabethans of the influence of supernatural powers, e.g. fairies (*Hamlet*, I. 1. 163); cf. Cotgrave (1611), "*fée*, taken, bewitched." Hence 'to charm, fascinate'—as in *Com.* 558; cf. Tennyson's *Dying Swan*, III.:

"The wild swan's death-hymn took the soul
    Of that waste place."

Cf. the colloquial use now of ' taking ' = ' charming.'

toy, *Com.* 502, 'a trifle.' Cf. *Macbeth*, II. 3. 99, "All is but toys." Cognate with Germ. *zeug*, 'stuff, trash,' as in *spielzeug*, 'playthings.'

trains, *Com.* 151, 'snares.' Cf. *Samson Agonistes*, 533, "venereal snares"=snares of love (Venus). F. *traîner*, from Lat. *trahere*, 'to draw,' in Late Lat. 'to betray'—from the metaphor of drawing birds into snares.

turkis, *Com.* 894, 'the turquoise,' literally 'Turkish stone.' Cf. Tennyson, *The Merman*, III., "Turkis and agate and almondine."

unharboured, *Com.* 423, 'yielding no *harbourage*, i.e. shelter.' A *harbinger* was originally an officer who went in advance of an army or prince to make provision for the night's shelter. From Icelandic *herbergi*, 'an army shelter'; cf. the cognate Germ. words *heer + bergen*. F. *auberge*, 'an inn,' is also from this Icelandic word.

usher, *Com.* 279. The noun (F. *huissier*, Lat. *ostiarius*) meant properly 'a doorkeeper,' later 'someone who went in front of any great person in a procession': hence the idea 'to precede, introduce.'

virtue, *Com.* 165, 'efficacy, power'; a frequent Elizabethan use. Cf. *Luke* viii. 46, "Virtue is gone out of me." So **virtuous**='full of efficacy' (*Com.* 621). Lat. *virtus*, 'worth, manly excellence' (Lat. *vir*, 'man').

wassailer, *Com.* 179, 'a reveller.' *Wassail* is the old northern English *wæs hǽl*, 'be whole'=the imperative of *wesan*, 'to be'+ *hǽl*, the same as *whole* and *hale*. Originally a salutation in drinking, like the Germ. *prosit!* ('may it benefit you'), used in drinking a man's health, *wassail* came to mean 'a drinking, carousing, revel.' Lady Macbeth promises to overcome the chamberlains "with wine and wassail" (I. 7. 64). The '*wassail-bowl*' was a great feature of the old Christmas feasting.

weed, *Com.* 16, 84, 390, 'garments, dress'; A.S. *wǽd*, 'a garment.' Commonly in the plural; cf. *Coriolanus*, II. 3. 161, "With a proud heart he wore his humble weeds." Now only in the phrase 'widow's weeds,' except in poetry; cf. Tennyson, "In words like weeds I'll wrap me o'er" (*In Memoriam*, V.).

welkin, *Com.* 1015, 'sky'; properly a plural word='clouds,' from A.S. *wolcnu*, the plural of *wolcen*, 'a cloud'; cf. Germ. *wolke*, 'a cloud.'

APPENDIX.

I.

THE ENGLISH MASQUE[1].

In the last years of the sixteenth century England owed much to Italian culture. For the age of Spenser Italy was what France a hundred years afterwards became for the age of Dryden, the great authority and model in everything pertaining to literature and art. It was from Italy that the Masque came. Hall tells us in the passage from his *Chronicle* quoted later on that the entertainment which struck people as so novel in 1512 was introduced "after the manner of Italie." Marlowe puts these lines into the mouth of Piers Gaveston, the favourite of Edward II.:

"I must have wanton poets, pleasant wits,
Musicians, that with touching of a string
May draw the pliant king which way I please:
Music and poetry is his delight;
Therefore I'll have Italian masks by night,
Sweet speeches, comedies, and pleasing shows."—
Edward II. i. 1.

In his *Chronicle History of the Stage*, pp. 22, 26, Mr Fleay notes that Italians "made pastime" for the Queen in 1574; that the Records of the Revels mention an Italian interpreter; and that the speeches of a Masque played before Elizabeth in 1579 were translated from English into Italian, at the Lord Chamberlain's direction.

---

[1] This sketch is mainly abridged from the longer account of the Masque prefixed to my first edition of *Comus*, where the various sources from which information is taken were mentioned. Anyone who desires to consult a fuller (and most interesting) account of the Masque should turn to Symonds' book, *Shakspere's Predecessors.*

There can be no question therefore as to the Italian origin of the Masque.

The earliest description of an English Masque occurs in Hall's *Chronicle* under the date 1512. He says:

"On the daie of the Epiphanie at night the King with xi other were disguised after the manner of Italie, called a maske, a thing not sene afore in England: thei were appareled in garments long and brode, wrought all with golde, with visers and cappes of gold; and after the banket doen these Maskers came in with the sixe gentlemen disguised in silke, beryng staffe-torches, and desired the ladies to daunce: some were content, and some that knew the fashion of it refused, because it was not a thing commonly seen. And after thei daunced and communed together, as the fashion of the maskes is, thei toke their leave and departed; and so did the Queene and all the ladies."

The entertainment thus described was what we should call a 'masquerade': an entertainment, that is, in which 'masks' or vizards were worn and dances were the chief element. Often the dances were supposed to illustrate some story, as it were in 'dumb show,' and gradually allegorical characters, e.g. Love, were brought in to explain the story to the audience, and songs were introduced. Hence from being merely a series of dances performed by masked characters, the Masque came to be a kind of play which was accompanied by a good deal of music and therefore resembled an opera. Scenery was then required, and wealthy patrons of the Masque vied with each other in the splendour of their representations. Here the Masque was influenced by the Pageant. The latter was of even older origin. Mention is made as early as 1236 of the City-pageants celebrated in London by members of the trade guilds. Of these spectacular processions, representing symbolically the various trades, which passed through the London streets at great festivities, the Lord Mayor's Show is a survival. Sometimes, e.g. in Shirley's great Masque *The Triumph of Peace*, a procession formed the introduction to a Masque; and the general influence of the Pageant was to foster a taste for spectacular display. This taste was not gratified in the public theatres simply because the theatrical managers could not afford the expense. But it was gratified in the Masque-performances given by the Court, great nobles, and the four legal societies

(Inner Temple, Middle Temple, Gray's Inn and Lincoln's Inn), whose Christmas-tide festivities or 'Revels[1]' were of a costly description.

Gradually therefore the Masque developed from its simple origin as a masquerade into a complex form of entertainment scarcely distinguishable from an opera.

The Masque reached its zenith in the reign of James I. Ben Jonson was the great master of the art, and his Masques may be taken as specimens of the finest type. They present these features:

The characters are deities of classical mythology, nymphs and personified qualities such as 'Love,' 'Harmony,' 'Delight,' 'Laughter' (for throughout its history the Masque preserved a marked strain of allegory). The number of characters seldom exceeds six, and there are generally two bands to whom the title 'Masquers' is specially assigned and who serve as choruses, now separately and in contrast, now in union. Thus in the *Masque of Hymen* there are eight maidens personifying the powers exercised by Juno in her capacity of patroness of women in wedlock, and eight knights personifying the 'Humours' and 'Affections' of man. In the *Masque of Queens* there are twelve witches embodying evil qualities, such as 'Ignorance,' 'Suspicion,' and against them are set twelve queens representing the highest fame. The scenes are laid in ideal regions—Olympus, Arcadia, the Fortunate Isles, the Palace of Oceanus, and similar realms of fancy. The length of the pieces, of course, varies, but the average Masque is about equal to the first Act of *The Tempest*. They are written in various metres of rhymed verse, which is sometimes spoken, sometimes declaimed in recitative, and contain solos for the chief characters and part-songs and choruses.

Dances, executed by the 'Masquers,' are a very important element: stately 'measures,' 'corantos,' 'galliards,' and the like, of Italian or French origin, and all new to England. Most elaborate scenery is employed, giving the representations a highly spectacular character, and the dresses of the performers are of the costliest description and symbolical. It is interesting, in passing, to remember the contrast between the bare simplicity

---

[1] *Twelfth Night* was acted at the Candlemas feast (Jan. 6) of the Middle Temple in 1602.

which characterised the representation of Shakespeare's pieces at the Globe Theatre[1] and the rich display of the Masque.

Generally there is a comic part called the Anti-masque. This serves as a contrast to the idealism of the Masque itself. It is a foil, an opposite: hence its name. Sometimes the Anti-masque consists of a scene or two of humorous dialogue and action, which have a satirical relation to the main subject and almost parody it; the characters being drawn from contemporary Elizabethan life. Sometimes the Anti-masque is merely a grotesque interlude. One moment personifications of Delight, and Harmony, and Love move across the scene, chanting some rhythmic choral strain to a slow recitative: the next all is confusion: the Anti-masquers rush forward, grotesque in dress and movement, execute fantastic dances and movements, and retire.

Milton does not attempt to work out an Anti-masque in *Comus*, very wisely, as he had little humour in his nature. But it may be conjectured that had Ben Jonson been the author of *Comus* at least two episodes in the poem would have been treated as burlesque interludes. These would have occurred at line 93, where Comus first appears, and at line 957: the Anti-masquers being in the one case the "rout of monsters," and in the other the "Country Dancers," with their clumsy "ducks and nods."

We have nothing in our own day that corresponds precisely with the Masque of the reign of James I. It was like an opera, because so much music was introduced; like a ballet, because there was so much dancing; like a pageant, because the scenery, setting and costumes were devised on so splendid a scale. It was certainly the forerunner of the opera, and composers like Lawes and Lock, to whom we owe our earliest operas, had in their youth written the incidental music of the latest Masques.

The Masque was a private form of entertainment, much patronised by the Court of James I. The Laureate Ben Jonson would write the *libretto*; the Court-composer Alfonso Ferrabosco often furnished the music, which would be rendered by the Court-orchestra and the choirs of the Chapels Royal; and the Court-architect, Inigo Jones, designed the scenery. Great nobles too, as we have said, and the legal societies gave Masque-performances. The Masque was peculiarly suited to be a form

---

[1] Cf. the first Prologue to *Henry V*.

of private theatricals because little skill in acting was required. The Queen and her maids of honour and courtiers could render the songs and execute the dances and rhythmic movements with all due effect, and satisfy the slender demands on their skill as players; though professional actors were sometimes employed for the Anti-masque, and professional musicians (usually the singers at the Chapels Royal) when the solo parts presented great difficulty.

Great ceremonies and occasions were signalised by Masque-performances, such as the Twelfth Night festivities at Whitehall, royal visits to noblemen's houses and weddings. Of course, the subject and allegory of a Masque were suited to the occasion for which it was composed. Thus in a Wedding-Masque the characters are Juno, Venus, Hymen, the Graces, etc., powers whose blessing is invoked on the wedded pair. And there is often, as in *Comus*, an element of personal compliment and local allusion.

The Masque declined somewhat on the death of James in 1625. Charles I. indeed was equally devoted to amusements. He was a good actor. As a boy he had played in several of Jonson's pieces, and *Love's Triumph through Callipolis* (1630) was performed "by his Majesty, with the Lords and Gentlemen Assisting." But the novelty was gone. An art or taste which depends on the whims of wealth and fashion has no element of permanence: what is in vogue to-day is voted obsolete to-morrow. Moreover the Masque had become too costly. We are told that Daniel's Masque *Hymen's Triumph* cost about £3000; Jonson's *Masque of Blackness* also about £3000, and his *Hue and Cry of Cupid* nearly £4000; while the expense of producing Shirley's *Triumph of Peace* reached the fabulous amount of £21,000 (which we must multiply by 4 to get its modern equivalent).

Entertainments which swallowed up a sum equivalent to the revenue of a small country could not be matters of frequent occurrence, especially when the royal purse was none too full. Moreover, as literature, the Masque had suffered inevitably by the mania for elaborate scenery, dresses and the like features of representation. Ben Jonson indeed insisted that the words were the real life and *anima* of the Masque: that the poetry should have the place of honour, and the other arts—music, sculpture, painting—serve as her handmaids. But this was not the popular view. Even his contemporary and fellow writer of Masques, Daniel in the preface to the *Masque of Tethys* declared that the poet's share in a Masque was "the least...and of least note: the only life consists in show, the art and invention of the architect gives the greatest graces, and is of the most importance."

The Masque in fact has come to be regarded as merely a peg whereon to hang costly extravagance. "Painting and carpentry are the soul of Masque" was Ben Jonson's final and bitterly ironical summing up of the whole matter. Just so nowadays a piece may attract by the splendour of its stage-spectacle rather than by any merit in the drama itself.

Curiously enough, when the period of its decadence was far advanced the Masque had a sudden and passing revival of life. This happened just before the composition of *Comus*. "In 1633 the Puritan hatred to the theatre had blazed out in Prynne's *Histriomastix*, and as a natural consequence, the loyal and cavalier portion of society threw itself into dramatic amusements of every kind. It was an unreal revival of the Mask, stimulated by political passion, in the wane of genuine taste for the fantastic and semi-barbarous pageant, in which the former age had delighted"—(Mark Pattison). This revival was marked by the production of the famous Masque already mentioned, Shirley's *Triumph of Peace*, and of Carew's *Cælum Britannicum*. The former was acted on Feb. 3, 1634, by the four legal societies, who desired, says a writer of that period, to express thereby "their love and duty to their majesties...and to manifest the difference of their opinion from Mr Prynne's new learning." Carew's Masque was given by the Court a fortnight later. Probably Milton was then busy with the composition of *Comus*, acted some months after. Each of these Masques has some association with *Comus*, as Lawes wrote the music for each, while two of the performers in the *Cælum Britannicum* were Viscount Brackley and Mr Thomas Egerton, the "Brothers" of Milton's Masque. The occasional representations of Masques after the Restoration, and even in this century, have merely an antiquarian interest. As a form of dramatic art the Masque lost its identity in the opera.

Ben Jonson's primacy in masque-writing stands unchallenged, but the art counted other distinguished exponents—e.g. Beaumont and Fletcher; Dekker and Middleton, who wrote city-pageants; Daniel, Chapman and Marston, patronised mainly by the Court and nobles ; and Shirley and Carew, the representatives of its waning glories.

Nor was Shakespeare uninfluenced by the Masque. *A Midsummer-Night's Dream* is rather a Masque-comedy than comedy proper. The classical characters and locality, the supernatural beings, the picturesque scenery required, the fanciful story, the rhymed and various types of verse, the large element of music and dance, the comic "interlude" of Bottom and his friends, who not only serve as contrasts to the classical characters of Theseus and his courtiers and to the fairies, but also parody in their "tragical mirth" the love-element of the serious scenes : all these are features in which Shakespeare's play reveals its kinship with the Masque. The pageant of Hymen in *As You Like It*, v. 4, is an episode which might have been detached from an ordinary Masque; and so is the Vision in *Cymbeline*, v. 4. The Masquerade in *Henry VIII.* I. 4, reminds us of the simple type of Masque described by Hall. The Masque in the fourth Act of *The Tempest*, though brief, contains the characteristic features. The theme is an allegory of marriage-bliss. The characters are taken from mythology. The Nymphs and Reapers represent the bands of 'Masquers.' Their dresses[1] are emblematical. There are songs, a "graceful dance," music. The verse is rhymed and varied. And the interlude akin to a Masque in the third Act, scene 3, illustrates the use of scenery and stage-machinery.

II.

"SABRINA FAIR": *Comus*, 824—842.

The story of Sabrina, the "nymph" of the Severn, had been previously told by several poets: by Drayton in the *Polyolbion*, Sixth Song, by Warner in *Albion's England*, and Spenser in *The Faerie Queene*, II. 10. 14—19, and in the old play *Locrine* (absurdly attributed at one time to Shakespeare). The first presentment, however, of the legend occurs in the Latin History of the Britons by Geoffrey of Monmouth (made Bishop of St Asaph in 1152). This Milton reproduced in his own prose History of England. He relates how Brutus the great-grandson of Æneas, landed in Albion, built Troja Nova

---

[1] Thus the "Nymphs" of the brooks are bidden to come with their "sedged crowns," IV. 129, sedge being symbolical of water-deities (cf. *Lyc.* 104), and the "Reapers" are "properly habited" (Stage-direction).

(afterwards called Trinovantum=London), and at his death divided his territory between Locrine, Albanact, and Camber, his three sons. Locrine later on defeated Humber, king of the Huns, who had invaded Britain, and, says Milton, "among the spoils of his camp and navy were found certain young maids, and Estrildis above the rest, passing fair, the daughter of a king in Germany; whom Locrine, though before contracted to the daughter of Corineus [a Trojan warrior who accompanying Brutus to Britain had received Cornwall], resolves to marry. But being forced and threatened by Corineus, whose authority and power he feared, Guendolen the daughter he yields [consents] to marry, but in secret he loves the other [Estrildis]: and......had by her a daughter equally fair, whose name was Sabra. But when once his fear was off by the death of Corineus, divorcing Guendolen, he makes Estrildis now his queen. Guendolen, all in rage, departs into Cornwall, where Madan, the son she had by Locrine, was hitherto brought up by Corineus his grandfather. And gathering an army of her father's friends and subjects, gives battle to her husband by the river Sture [i.e. Stour]; wherein Locrine, shot with an arrow, ends his life. But not so ends the fury of Guendolen: for Estrildis, and her daughter Sabra, she throws into a river: and, to leave a monument of revenge, proclaims that the stream be thenceforth called after the damsel's name; which, by length of time, is changed now to Sabrina, or Severn"—*P. W.* v. 173, 174.

Cf. Spenser (II. 10. 19) describing how Guendolen, having taken "the faire Sabrina" (cf. *Comus*, 859) and her mother prisoners, slew the latter,

> "But the sad Virgin, innocent of all,
>
> Adoune the rolling river she did poure,
>
> Which of her name now Severne men do call:
>
> Such was the end that to disloyall love did fall."

So also at the close of the play *Locrine* (v. 5), where Sabren drowns herself, and Guendolen says:

> "because this river was the place
>
> Where little Sabren resolutely died,
>
> Sabren for ever shall this stream be call'd."

Milton had hinted at the legend previously; cf. the *Vacation Exercise*, 96, "Or Severn swift, guilty of maiden's death."

CRITICAL OPINIONS ON COMUS.

"The greatest of his juvenile performances is the 'Masque of Comus,' in which may very plainly be discovered the dawn or twilight of *Paradise Lost*. Milton appears to have formed very early that system of diction, and mode of verse, which his maturer judgment approved, and from which he never endeavoured nor desired to deviate.

Nor does *Comus* afford only a specimen of his language; it exhibits likewise his power of description and his vigour of sentiment, employed in the praise and defence of virtue. A work more truly poetical is rarely found; allusions, images, and descriptive epithets, embellish almost every period with lavish decoration. As a series of lines, therefore, it may be considered as worthy of all the admiration with which the votaries have received it.

As a drama it is deficient. The action is not probable. A masque, in those parts where supernatural intervention is admitted, must indeed be given up to all the freaks of imagination, but so far as the action is merely human, it ought to be reasonable, which can hardly be said of the conduct of the two brothers; who, when their sister sinks with fatigue in a pathless wilderness, wander both away together in search of berries too far to find their way back, and leave a helpless lady to all the sadness and danger of solitude. This, however, is a defect overbalanced by its convenience.

What deserves more reprehension is, that the prologue spoken in the wild wood by the attendant Spirit is addressed to the audience; a mode of communication so contrary to the nature of dramatic representation, that no precedents can support it.

The discourse of the Spirit is too long; an objection that may be made to almost all the following speeches; they have not the sprightliness of a dialogue animated by reciprocal contention, but seem rather declamations deliberately composed, and formally repeated, on a moral question. The auditor therefore listens as to a lecture, without passion, without anxiety.

The song of Comus has airiness and jollity; but, what may recommend Milton's morals as well as his poetry, the invitations to pleasure are so general, that they excite no distinct images of corrupt enjoyment, and take no dangerous hold on the fancy.

The following soliloquies of Comus and the Lady are elegant but tedious. The song must owe much to the voice, if it ever can delight. At last the Brothers enter with too much tranquillity; and, when they have feared lest their Sister should be in danger, and hoped that she is not in danger, the elder makes a speech in praise of chastity, and the younger finds how fine it is to be a philosopher.

Then descends the Spirit in form of a shepherd; and the Brother, instead of being in haste to ask his help, praises his singing, and inquires his business in that place. It is remarkable, that at this interview the Brother is taken with a short fit of rhyming. The Spirit relates that the Lady is in the power of Comus; the Brother moralises again; and the Spirit makes a long narration, of no use because it is false, and therefore unsuitable to a good being.

In all these parts the language is poetical, and the sentiments are generous; but there is something wanting to allure attention.

The dispute between the Lady and Comus is the most animated and affecting scene of the drama, and wants nothing but a brisker reciprocation of objections and replies to invite attention, and detain it.

The songs are vigorous and full of imagery; but they are harsh in their diction, and not very musical in their numbers.

Throughout the whole the figures are too bold, and the

language too luxuriant for dialogue. It is a drama in the epic style, inelegantly splendid, and tediously instructive."

[MACAULAY: *ESSAY ON MILTON.*]

"Milton attended in the *Comus* to the distinction which he afterwards neglected in the *Samson* [*Agonistes*]. He made his Masque what it ought to be, essentially lyrical, and dramatic only in semblance. He has not attempted a fruitless struggle against a defect inherent in the nature of that species of composition; and he has therefore succeeded, wherever success was not impossible. The speeches must be read as majestic soliloquies; and he who so reads them will be enraptured with their eloquence, their sublimity, and their music. The interruptions of the dialogue, however, impose a constraint upon the writer, and break the illusion of the reader. The finest passages are those which are lyric in form as well as in spirit. 'I should much commend,' says the excellent Sir Henry Wotton in a letter to Milton, 'the tragical part if the lyrical did not ravish me with a certain dorique delicacy in your songs and odes, whereunto, I must plainly confess to you, I have seen yet nothing parallel in our language.' The criticism was just. It is when Milton escapes from the shackles of the dialogue, when he is discharged from the labour of uniting two incongruous styles, when he is at liberty to indulge his choral raptures without reserve, that he rises even above himself. Then, like his own good genius bursting from the earthly form and weeds of Thyrsis, he stands forth in celestial freedom and beauty."

[HALLAM: *LITERATURE OF EUROPE.*]

"*Comus* was sufficient to convince anyone of taste and feeling that a great poet had arisen in England, and one partly formed in a different school from his contemporaries. Many of them had produced highly beautiful and imaginative passages; but none had evinced so classical a judgment, none had aspired to so regular a perfection. Johnson had learned much from the ancients; but there was a grace in their best models which he did not quite attain. Neither his *Sad Shepherd* nor the *Faithful Shepherdess* of Fletcher has the elegance or dignity of

Comus. A noble virgin and her young brothers, by whom this masque was originally represented, required an elevation, a purity, a sort of severity of sentiment, which no one in that age could have given but Milton. He avoided, and nothing loath, the more festive notes which dramatic poetry was wont to mingle with its serious strain. But for this he compensated by the brightest hues of fancy and the sweetest melody of song. In *Comus* we find nothing prosaic or feeble, no false taste in the incidents, and not much in the language, nothing ever which we should desire to pass on a second perusal. The want of what we may call personality, none of the characters having names, except Comus himself, who is a very indefinite being, and the absence of all positive attributes of time and place, entrance the ideality of the fiction by a certain indistinctness not unpleasing to the imagination."

[BAGEHOT: LITERARY STUDIES.]

"The power of *Comus* is in its style. A grave and firm music pervades it : it is soft, without a thought of weakness; harmonious, and yet strong ; impressive, as few such poems are, yet covered with a bloom of beauty and a complexity of charm that few poems have either. We have, perhaps, light literature in itself better, that we read oftener and more easily, that lingers more in our memories; but we have not any, we question if there ever will be any, which gives so true a conception of the capacity and the dignity of the mind by which it was produced. The breath of solemnity which hovers round the music attaches us to the writer. Every line, here as elsewhere, in Milton excites the idea of indefinite power."

[R. GARNETT: LIFE OF MILTON.]

"*Comus*, the richest fruit of Milton's early genius, is the epitome of the man at the age at which he wrote it. It bespeaks the scholar and idealist, whose sacred enthusiasm is in some danger of contracting a taint of pedantry for want of acquaintance with men and affairs. The Elder Brother's dialogues with his junior reveal the same solemn insensibility to the humorous which characterises the kindred genius of Wordsworth, and would have provoked the kindly smile of Shakespeare. It is singular to find the inevitable flaw of *Paradise Lost* prefigured here, and the wicked enchanter made the real hero of the piece. These defects are interesting, because they represent the nature of Milton as it was then, noble and disinterested to the height of imagination, but self-assertive, unmellowed, angular. They disappear entirely when he expatiates in the regions of exalted fancy, as in the introductory discourse of the Spirit, and the invocation to Sabrina. They recur when he moralizes ; and his morality is too interwoven with the texture of his piece to be other than obtrusive. What glorious morality it is no one need be told; nor is there any poem in the language where beauties of thought, diction, and description spring up more thickly than in *Comus*... It is, indeed, true that many of these jewels are fetched from the mines of other poets: great as Milton's obligations to Nature were, his obligations to books were greater. But he has made all his own by the alchemy of his genius, and borrows little but to improve."

[DOWDEN: *TRANSCRIPTS AND STUDIES.*]

"*Comus* is the work of a youthful spirit, enamoured of its ideals of beauty and of virtue, zealous to exhibit the identity of moral loveliness with moral severity. The real incident[1] from which the mask is said to have originated disengages itself, in the imagination of Milton, from the world of actual occurrences, and becomes an occasion for the dramatic play of his own poetical abstractions. The young English gentlemen cast off their identity and individuality, and appear in the elementary shapes of 'First Brother' and 'Second Brother.' The Lady Alice rises into an ideal impersonation of virgin strength and virtue. The scene is earth; a wild wood; but earth, as in all the poems of Milton, with the heavens arching over it—a dim spot, in which men 'strive to keep up a frail and feverish being' set below the 'starry threshold of Love's Court.'... From its first scene to the last the drama is a representation of the trials, difficulties, and dangers to which moral purity is exposed in this

---

[1] Referring to the popular but very doubtful tradition as to the genesis of *Comus* ; see the *Introduction*.

world, and of the victory of the better principle in the soul, gained by strenuous human endeavour aided by the grace of God. In this spiritual warfare the powers of good and evil are arrayed against one another; upon this side the Lady, her brothers (types of human helpfulness weak in itself, and liable to go astray), and the supernatural powers auxiliar to virtue in heaven and in earth—the Attendant Spirit and the nymph Sabrina.

The enchanter Comus is son of Bacchus and Circe, and inheritor of twofold vice. If Milton had pictured the life of innocent mirth in *L'Allegro*, here was a picture to set beside the other, a vision of the genius of sensual indulgence. Yet Comus is inwardly, not outwardly foul; no grim monster like that which the mediæval imagination conjured up to terrify the spirit and disgust the senses. The attempt of sin upon the soul as conceived by Milton is not the open and violent obsession of a brute power, but involves a cheat, an imposture. The soul is put upon its trial through the seduction of the senses and the lower parts of our nature. Flattering lies entice the ears of Eve[1]; Christ is tried[2] by false visions of power and glory, and beneficent rule; Samson is defrauded of his strength by deceitful blandishment[3]. And in like manner Comus must needs possess a beauty of his own, such beauty as ensnares the eye untrained in the severe school of moral perfection....He is sensitive to rich forms and sweet sounds, graceful in oratory, possessed, like Satan, of high intellect, but intellect in the service of the senses; he surrounds himself with a world of art which lulls the soul into forgetfulness of its higher instincts and of duty; his palace is stately, and 'set out with all manner of deliciousness.'

Over against this potent enchanter stands the virginal figure of the Lady, who is stronger than he... Something of weakness belongs to the Lady, because she is a woman, accustomed to the protection of others, tenderly nurtured; but when the hour of trial comes she shows herself strong in powers of judgment and of reasoning, strong in her spiritual nature, in her tenacity of moral truth, in her indignation against sin. Although alone, and encompassed by evil and danger, she is fearless, and so

---

[1] *Paradise Lost*, IX. 532—732. [2] *Paradise Regained*, III. IV.
[3] *Samson Agonistes*, 392—411.

clear-sighted that the juggling practice of her antagonist is
wholly ineffectual against her.   There is much in the Lady
which resembles the youthful Milton himself, and we may well
believe that the great debate concerning temperance was not
altogether dramatic (where, indeed, is Milton truly dramatic?),
but was in part a record of passages in the poet's own spiritual
history.   Milton admired the Lady as he admired the ideal
which he projected before him of himself."

POLITICAL AND SOCIAL ASPECTS OF MILTON'S EARLY POEMS.

[STOPFORD BROOKE: "*CLASSICAL WRITERS*," *MILTON*.]

" Puritanism, when Milton began to write, was not universally
apart from literature and the fine arts.   In its staid and pure
religion Milton's work had its foundation, but the temple he had
begun to build upon it was quarried from the ancient and modern
arts and letters of Greece and Italy and England.   And filling
the temple rose the peculiar incense of the Renaissance.   The
breath of that spirit is felt in the classicalism of the *Ode to the
Nativity*, in the love proclaimed for Shakespeare, in the graceful
fancy of the *Epitaph to Lady Winchester*, and in the gaiety of
the *Ode to a May Morning*.   But a new element, other than
any the Renaissance could produce, is here ; the element that
filled the Psalms of David, the deep, personal, passionate religion
of the Puritan, possessing, and possessed by, God.   Over against
the Renaissance music is set the high and devout strain of the
first sonnet and of the *Odes to Time* and *A Solemn Musick*.   Even
while at Cambridge, the double being in Milton makes itself felt,
the struggle between the two spirits of the time is reflected in his
work.   These contrasted spirits in him became defined as the
political and social war deepened around his life.   The second
sonnet still is gay, fresh with the morn of love, Petrarca might
have written it ; the *Allegro* does not disdain the love of nature,

the rustic sports, the pomp of courts, the playhouse and the land of faery, nor does the *Penseroso* refuse to haunt the dim cathedral. But yet, in these two poems more than in the Cambridge poems, the deepening of the struggle is felt. Milton seems to presage in them that the time would come when the gaiety of England would cease to be shared in by serious men; when the mirth of the Cavalier would shut out the pleasures derived from lofty Melancholy, because they shut out the devil; as the Puritan pensiveness would be driven to shut out the pleasures of Mirth, because they shut out God. While he gives full weight in the *Allegro* to 'unreproved pleasures free,' he makes it plain in the *Penseroso* that he prefers the sage and holy pleasures of thoughtful sadness. These best befitted the solemn aspect of the time.

A few years later and the presage had come true. Milton is driven away from even the *Allegro* point of view. In *Comus* the wild licence of the Court society is set over against the grave and temperate virtue of a Puritan life. The unchastity, the glozing lies, the glistering apparel that hid moral deformity, the sloth and drunkenness, the light fantastic round of the enchanter's character and court, are (it seems likely) Milton's allegory of the Court society of his time. The stately philosophy of the Brothers which had its root in subduing passion and its top in the love of God; the virginal chastity of the Lady, and at the end the releasing power of Sabrina's purity, exalt and fill up more sternly the idea of the *Penseroso* and symbolise that noble Puritanism which loved learning and beauty only when they were pure, but holiness far more than either. It may be, as Mr Browne supports, that there is a second allegory within the first, of Laud and his party as the Sorcerer commending the cup of Rome by wile and threat to the lips of the Church and enforcing it by fine and imprisonment; paralysing in stony fetters the Lady of the Church. It may be that Milton called in this poem on the few who, having resisted like the Brothers, but failed to set the Church free, ought now to employ a new force, the force of Purity; but this aspect of the struggle is at least not so clear in *Comus* as in *Lycidas*.

In *Lycidas* Milton has thrown away the last shreds of Church and State and is Presbyterian. The strife now at hand starts into prominence, and not to the bettering of the poem as a piece of art. It is brought in—and the fault is one which frequently startles us in Milton—without any regard to the unity of feeling in the poem. The passage on the hireling Church looks like an after-thought, and Milton draws attention to it in the argument. 'The author...by occasion foretells the ruin of our corrupted clergy then in their height.' But he does not leave Laud and his policy nor the old Church tenderly. When he felt strongly, he wrote fiercely. The passage is a splendid and a fierce cry of wrath, and the rough trumpet note, warlike and unsparing, which it sounds against the unfaithful herdsmen who are sped and the 'grim wolf with privy paw,' was to ring louder and louder through the prose works, and finally to clash in the ears of those very Presbyterians whom he now supported.

There is then a steady progress of thought and of change in the poems. The Milton of *Lycidas* is not the Milton of *Comus*. The Milton of *Comus* is not the Milton of the *Penseroso*, less still of the *Allegro*. The Milton of the *Penseroso* is not the Milton of the *Ode to the Nativity*. Nothing of the Renaissance is left now but its learning and its art."